James L. Ford

The Third Alarm

A story of the New York Fire Department, with an introduction on the life and career of John James Bresnan, a batallion chief of the New York City Fire Department

James L. Ford

The Third Alarm
A story of the New York Fire Department, with an introduction on the life and career of John James Bresnan, a batallion chief of the New York City Fire Department

ISBN/EAN: 9783337256760

Printed in Europe, USA, Canada, Australia, Japan

Cover: Foto ©ninafisch / pixelio.de

More available books at **www.hansebooks.com**

THE THIRD ALARM

A STORY OF THE NEW YORK FIRE
DEPARTMENT

BY
JAMES L. FORD
Author of " Hypnotic Tales," " Dr. Doad's School," etc.

New York
BRENTANO'S
CHICAGO   PARIS   WASHINGTON

This Book

Is DEDICATED BY ITS AUTHOR

TO

A NEW YORK FIREMAN,

JOHN J. BRESNAN,

Chief of Sixth Battalion, N. Y. F. D

List of Illustrations.

	PAGE
"Well my boy what can I do for you?" *Frontispiece*	
"Well, Pete, old fellow, I've heard of you many a time."	8
Chief Trask explains the fire box to Bruce.	17
"For fully a minute Bruce stood looking at the house."	47
Bruce tells Laura the story of his visit to Mr. Dexter's house.	72
Bruce in Mr. Dewsnap's "fire library."	79
"Never in his life had Bruce known such a reckless ride."	91
"She was certainly very deaf."	98
Bruce delivers a lecture on botany.	122
"Did you get the beggars' time?"	136
"He managed to climb out on the ladder."	156
Laura visits Bruce in the hospital.	190
Then Laura began to cry.	202
"So you've been in the hospital, have you?"	225
"My mother is buried here."	248
"Mr. Dexter * * * held out his hand for the address."	257
"Dere's an answer ter dat."	286
"And so this is the business you conduct, is it?"	317
"The horses bounded to their places."	343
"A single slip or false step on his part meant death."	368

THE THIRD ALARM.

CHAPTER I.

"DO you see that boy sitting on the curbstone over the way? Well, he's been there for the last half hour, and I'd just like to know what he's up to. Run over, Charley, and ask him what he wants."

It was John Trask, a chief of battalion in the New York Fire Department who addressed these words to his subordinate, Charley Weyman, one pleasant afternoon in early spring, and the boy to whom he referred had been sitting for some time on the curbstone across the street from the hook and ladder company's quarters, peering anxiously through the open door which afforded him a view of the hook and ladder truck, the horses quietly munching their hay, and, in the rear room, half a dozen firemen seated about a table talking, reading or playing checkers.

The boy, who seemed to be about fifteen years of age, looked as if he had just reached town after a long and weary walk. His clothes were torn and travel-stained, and there was a gaunt, hungry look in his face that spoke unmistakeably of want and privation. It was this look and the boy's dejected attitude which had first attracted the chief's attention for he feared that he might be waiting for a chance to get into the building, and steal what he could lay his hands on.

"There's something queer about that kid," he continued, half to himself, as he watched Weyman cross the street and enter into conversation with him. "Hulloa! he's bringing him over here; he must want to see somebody," and just then the fireman entered leading the boy with him.

"He says he wants to see you, chief," said Weyman, seating himself in an arm-chair while the boy stood with his hat in his hand waiting respectfully for the other to address him.

"Well, my boy," said the chief of battalion in a kindly voice, "what can I do for you?"

"Are you Mr. John Trask, chief of the battalion?" inquired the boy.

"I am" was the reply.

"Well, did you ever have a man here in the company named Frank Decker?"

At the mention of this name a sudden silence fell upon the little group of men who were gathered about the table, newspapers were laid aside, the talking ceased, and every eye was turned on the hungry looking, travel-stained boy who stood with his hat in his hand, looking the chief squarely in the face while he put the question.

The chief paused a moment as he adjusted a pair of eye-glasses on his nose, and then answered in a voice that had something of a stern soldierly ring in it: "I knew Frank Decker well, and I wish there were more men on the earth like him. But what have you to do with Frank Decker?"

"My name is Bruce Decker and Frank Decker was my father" replied the boy, still looking the chief squarely in the eye and trying to speak steadily, but there was a little break in his voice as he mentioned his father's name and a faint quiver in his lower lip as he finished.

"Frank Decker's boy!" exclaimed Weyman springing to his feet, "Why I never knew he had a boy!"

"Where do you come from, young man?" inquired Chief Trask, regarding him now with a new interest and shifting his position so as to get a clear view of the young lad's face.

"I come from Oswego County way back in the state, where I've lived all my life. I got here early this morning and came here because

I had no other place to go to. I've never been in New York before, but father used to tell me about you and a friend of his named Mr. Weyman and so I thought maybe you'd be willing to give me a lift, if only on his account."

"Upon my word I believe the boy is speaking the truth, "said Chief Trask;" he's got Frank's nose and eyes and his straight way of looking at you and—here just turn around a moment, my boy—yes, there it is, that little patch of gray on the back of his head that Frank used to tell us was the birth mark of every Decker that ever was born. Well young man—Bruce you say your name is? I'm glad to see you, and what's more I'll be glad to help you, if you need help. Here, give me your hand and sit down beside me."

Bruce seated himself beside his new friend and then Weyman stepped over and whispered something in the chief's ear.

"Certainly!" exclaimed that official hastily," come along with me, boy, and have something to eat; it's just about dinner time."

As the two left the truck house the others laid aside their newspapers and games and began an eager discussion of the new arrival, whose father had been, until his death three months before, a member of the company.

"I heard once that he had a boy somewhere up the country," said Tom Brophy, and I've no doubt this lad is just what he claims to be, the son of Frank Decker, because he resembles him in every particular, And if he is Frank's son why we ought to see to it that he has a fair chance to get along here, and not turn him adrift—to make out as best he can. We're not one of us rich, but we're not so poor that we can't spare a dollar now and then for a son of one of the squarest and best men that the department ever had."

Brophy's words were received with a degree of enthusiasm and approval that showed plainly that he and his comrades were of one mind as to the course they should pursue in welcoming and looking after the son of their old friend, and until the return of the boy and Chief Trask, they sat talking over the days when Frank Decker was one of the quickest, bravest and most popular men in all the department.

But before proceeding any further with our story, it will be necessary to turn back to the time about twelve years before the appearance of Bruce Decker at the door of the New York truck house, when Frank Decker, a strong, hearty, active man of twenty-five, turned his back on the little village near Lake Ontario, where he had just buried his young wife, and, having placed his little boy in the care of some distant relatives, set out for the city in the hope of beginning anew a career which had been broken by financial misfortune and the loss of his wife. Through the influence of an old friend he had obtained an appointment in the fire department, in which service he had distinguished himself by his bravery, coolness and zeal, qualities which served to commend him to the notice of the chief officers of the department, and which would probably have won for him a place at the head of a battalion, had it not been for the awful catastrophe at the burning of the Gothic Hotel on Broadway.

On this occasion Decker arrived, entered the hotel at the command of his chief, and ascended the staircase, in order to save some women who were supposed to be in one of the upper floors. That was the last seen of him, and late that night when the rest of his company had been relieved and were slowly making their way home, they spoke little of anything or anybody, save Frank Decker, who was among the missing and who had gone down before that awful sheet of flame that broke out and swept through the hotel about five minutes after he was seen to enter the building.

Half a dozen charred bodies were taken from the ruins the next day, but which one of them had once been Frank Decker no one could tell.

And while the father had been at work in the fire department, the child whom he had left in the little village in the northern part of the State, had grown in health, strength and mind, and was now in his sixteenth year, an active, vigorous, straightforward youth, who inherited all his father's daring and quickness, together with a willingness to learn and a decided taste for books, which had come to him direct from his mother.

During his short life he had cherished but one ambition, which was to become a fireman, and most of the correspondence which he always maintained with his father, had been in regard to the workings of the New York department, and particularly the battalion to which the elder belonged. Once a year the father had returned to his old home on the shore of the great fresh water lake to spend his short vacation with his boy, and during these visits it had been the habit of the two to take long walks and sails together, enjoying themselves after their own fashion, the boy listening with flushed cheeks and bated breath, while his father described to him the life of excitement and danger which he led as a member of what he always called. "the greatest fire department in the world."

From his father's lips the boy had heard stories of the swift runs to fires, of thrilling midnight rescues, of brave firemen plunging into solid sheets of smoke and flame, and so strong a hold had these stories taken on his mind that his desire to become a fireman himself had slowly grown within him, until it became the one fixed and cherished ambition of his life.

So it happened, naturally enough, that at his father's death he resolved to make his way to New York and ask John Trask, the chief of his father's old battalion, to appoint him to a place in the Department.

We have described in an earlier part of this chapter the arrival of Bruce Decker, footsore and travel-stained at the truck house, and his reception at the hands of the chief and his subordinates, and we left him going out for dinner under the guidance of his newly-made friend.

When he returned from the restaurant where he had enjoyed a hearty meal and a long, confidential talk with the chief, he stopped by the stalls in which the horses were standing, stroked the nose of the big gray, and said, without an instant's hesitation: "Well, Pete, old fellow,

"Well, Pete, old fellow, I've heard of you many a time."
Page 8.

I've heard of you many a time," and the horse laid his muzzle on the boy's shoulder and whinnied softly, as if he were returning the friendly greeting. The men noticed this and exchanged significant glances.

"Just like his father," said Weyman, in a low voice, "do you remember how fond Frank used to be of those horses? Why, he never came into the house without stopping to pet them."

"Well, my little man, how would you like to become a fireman? enquired Chief Trask, pleasantly, as he seated himself in his arm-chair and prepared to light his pipe. But before Bruce could answer, the sharp ring of the alarm bell echoed through the building and startled everyone into sudden activity.

Chapter II.

MANY a time had Frank Decker described, for the benefit of his boy, the rapidity with which his truck company would start for a fire at the stroke of the gong, but never had Bruce's imagination conceived of anything like that which took place now before his astonished eyes.

The electric current which sounded the alarm released the horses and the intelligent creatures sprang at once to their places beneath the harness that was suspended in midair from the ceiling of the room. Five of the men were at their heads at the same instant, while Weyman climbed into the driver's seat and took the reins in his hand and Brophy mounted behind and took his place at the steering apparatus. Two or three sharp clicks and the harness was adjusted, and then, while the rest of the company climbed recklessly over the wheels to their places on the truck, the horses bounded into the street, turned sharply to the left and dashed away in full gallop. Bruce rushed to the door and looked after the flying truck. Fully two blocks away he saw a man in fireman's uniform driving a galloping horse attached to a single seated wagon in which was a brass gong which he rang vigorously. It was Chief Trask leading the way to the fire.

Bruce went back to the room at the rear of the now deserted building and seated himself in one of the arm-chairs. His face was flushed, and he was trembling with excitement. If he had ever longed for a fireman's uniform he longed for it now, with an intensity such as he had never felt before, and he determined that no power on earth should prevent him entering the service and sustaining the reputation for courage and fidelity which his father had enjoyed for so many years.

That night Bruce Decker slept at the home of John Trask, and, while he was dreaming of fires and fire brigades and swift-moving horses, the chief and two or three of his men were gathered about a little round table at the rear of the truck house, discussing various schemes for giving the lad a start in the city.

"I don't know," said Charles Weyman, "but what the best thing we can do for the lad is to get him a job in some big store or place of business where he can begin at the beginning and work his way up There's nothing like business nowadays. Those big merchants make more money than any of the professional men do, when once they get a few thousand ahead, and anyway it's a great deal better than this fire department business, which is all risk and danger and excitement, with very little money to compensate for it. You know that he is entitled to a pension of $300 a year from the department, and that amount, together with what he could make as an office boy or young clerk, ought to keep him going. I know if I'd gone into business when I was his age I would have made a good deal more money than I have by running to fires."

"And yet you wouldn't change now if you had the chance would you?" said one of the men carelessly.

"No, I don't think I would—" began Weyman slowly, but Tom Brophy interrupted him with:

"What you say is all perfectly true, Charley, but you must remember one thing, and that is, that this lad is crazy over the Fire Department and anxious to get into it because his father was in it. Can't you see how much he's been thinking about it all his life? Did you notice how he recognized those horses and called them by name, just because his father had told him about them? Its very plain to me that all he's heard about the New York Fire Department has made a deep impression on him, and when a boy's got his head set on any particular line of business, it's very foolish to try and force him in any other direction. Let him have a try first at what inclination leads him to, and then if he finds out that it's not all a path of roses, it will be time enough for him to make a change and get into something else."

"But how are we going to get him started in the department yet awhile?" demanded Weyman. "You know the rules are, that no one under twenty-one years of age can be taken into the service, and this boy don't look to me to be more than fifteen. Get him into some good office now, and the chances are that by the time he's twenty-one he won't want to go to fires on a truck."

Then Chief Trask, who had been silent for some time, removed his pipe from his lips and said, in the authoritative way which was habitual with him: "If the boy wants to be a fireman I believe in giving him a chance. This pension of $300 a year ought to pay for his board and clothes and there are plenty of odd jobs he can do about the quarters while he's learning the business. He can make himself very useful to us here if he takes hold of the work in the right spirit, and if he gets sick of it within a year he won't be any the worse for his training."

That ended the discussion and very soon afterward the men went up stairs and turned in for the night.

The next morning the chief told Bruce that he had decided to give him employment for a few months in order that he might familiarize himself with the duties of a fireman. He could board at his (the chief's) home, and make himself generally useful at the quarters. "Do you know anything about taking care of horses?" he required.

"Yes," replied Bruce eagerly, "I've looked after horses all my life and I'd like nothing better than to take care of that big grey Pete that I've heard my father speak about so often. I am very handy with horses, and I can do anything with them. Then I'll run errands and do anything you want me to. I'd rather be a fireman than President of the United States."

Mr. Trask could not help smiling at the boy's earnestness, but it pleased him, nevertheless, to see that he was bent upon entering the service and did not intend to let a little hard work stand in the way of getting there. That very afternoon found Bruce with his coat off whistling merrily as he rubbed down the horses, Pete, Jack and Joe, and gave them their hay and oats. Charley Weyman watched him from his seat in the rear room, and remarked to Brophy: "That lad takes hold of his work as if he liked it.

Chapter III.

"HITCH up my wagon for me, Bruce," said the chief one morning a few days after the young boy had been installed at the quarters, and accordingly he harnessed one of the horses to the wagon which the chief kept for his own nse.

"Now jump in beside me," he continued, and a few minutes later they were driving slowly up the broad avenue, while the chief gave his young protege some information regarding the department.

"Remember this, my boy," he said earnestly, "that promptness and readiness are the watchwords of the service. Every second of time is of importance, and you should never let another man get ahead of you when you are getting ready to go to a fire, nor allow another company to get a stream on the fire first, if you can possibly prevent it. The paid department was established in 1865. I don't know how long it took an engine or truck to get out into the street then, but I do know that we have been lowering the record ever since, so that now the

Chief Trask explains the fire box to Bruce.—
Page 17.

average time from the first stroke of the alarm until the engine, manned and ready for action, passes over the threshold is not more than ten seconds, and it has been done, of course only for exhibition purposes, in two seconds. Not a year goes by but sees some new invention or improvement to facilitate the work of the department, and my own opinion is that the rivalry between the different companies is the strongest incentive to efficient work there is. Now I'll stop here and explain this fire box to you, so that you will be able to understand how these alarms come in." With these words, the chief drew up in front of a lamp-post which was painted a bright red and had red glass in its lamp. To this was attached the fire box from which any citizen could send an alarm of fire.

"Now," said the chief as he opened the box, "when a fire breaks out, anyone who discovers it runs to this box, or rather to the one nearest the scene of the conflagration, for you know these boxes are scattered all over the city, and turns this handle according to the printed directions. By pulling the hook down inside, the number of the box is telegraphed to the headquarters of the fire department, and the operator there sends another dispatch notifying the different engine houses in the immediate vicinity of the fire. This alarm comes in to us in the shape of sharp strokes, indicating the number of the alarm box. This is what we call a first alarm, and you will notice that there is a gong here in the box which rings when the handle is turned. That gong attracts the attention of the policeman on duty nearby, and he comes running up to find out where the fire is, or to arrest any person who may be ringing it maliciously.

"Once in a while the alarm is rung by some Irish servant girl who wants to send a letter back to the old country and mistakes this for a mail box. And once in a while it is rung by somebody who is deceived by a smoky chimney or a bonfire in a vacant lot. The other alarms intended to call out a greater force, can only be sent by an official, who has a key to the inside box. For example, suppose our company were to be called out to-night to a fire, and I were to find on arrival that it was in my own district, I would take command, even if another battalion chief were to be present also. In the same way he would take command, if the fire were in his district. But, suppose I find that the fire is a big one and in danger of spreading. I go to the box and sound the second alarm, which brings up an additional force. Then, suppose that I find the fire making such headway that we are unable to control it. Then I go to the box again and sound the third alarm, and that brings up every available engine and hook and ladder company within a reasonable distance. When that third alarm sounds in an engine house, every fireman knows that there's a big and dangerous fire to be fought, and every man goes out with a keener sense of his own responsibility than he would on an ordinary call."

"How often does the third alarm sound?" asked Bruce. who had been listening with intense interest to the chief's words.

"It's not very often that we have a fire big enough to warrant it," replied the official. "The last one we had was at an apartment house up town, about four months ago—"

He paused abruptly, remembering that it was at this fire that Frank Decker, the boy's father, had perished. And although Bruce said nothing, he knew what he meant.

Entering the wagon again, they drove a few blocks further and stopped in front of an engine house situated on a side street. A fireman, standing on the pavement in front of the door, saluted as the chief entered.

"Is Captain Murphy about?" asked the chief.

"Yes," replied the other, and then a tall, stoutly built man, with a military look and manner that corresponded well with his uniform, made his appearance from the rear room and bade his visitors welcome.

"This is Frank Decker's boy," said the chief, as he presented Bruce to the officer, "and we're going to try and make a fireman of him. I've brought him around here to show him what a fire engine is like."

"Frank Decker's boy!" exclaimed the captain, as he shook Bruce cordially by the hand.

"Well, all I can say is, you've got good material to work with. I knew Frank this twelve years or more, and a better fireman never rode on a tender."

"You see," said the chief, as he led the boy through the engine house, "this is a double company. That is to say, there's an engine and tender here to go out at the first alarm, and another to move up and take their places, so as to be ready in case an alarm comes in while the first company is off at the fire. Of course this engine that stands right here in front by the door is the one to go first, and its tender, or hose wagon as it used to be called in old times, goes with it. Then they move the second engine and tender right up to the front;

the second relay of horses drop down and take their places in the other stalls, and within two minutes after the alarm was first sounded, there is a complete equipment ready to go out to any other fires that may occur in the vicinity.

"Now I want you to notice the way this engine is kept ready for action at a second's notice. You see from the guage that there is twenty pounds pressure of steam in her boiler now, although there is no fire lit, and she has been standing here all day. That is because the steam is kept up from a fire in the basement, and the connection is made by these pipes that come up through the floor. The minute the engine starts, the connection with the pipes underneath is shut off automatically, and then as soon as the wheels cross the threshold of the building, the fire is lit, and as the swift motion of the street acts as a sort of draught, there is a big blaze going in less than two minutes. There's a little contrivance I want you to see, and although it may seem like a trivial one to you, it is really a very useful time-saving device."

As he said this, he took from a rack above the ash pan a pine stick about six inches long, around one end of which was wrapped a quantity of rags soaked in kerosene, from the midst of which protruded the heads of half a dozen matches.

"Now I'll explain to you," continued Chief Trask, "the value of this little torch. If we depended on matches, or took our chances of running to get a light from the gas-jet or anything like that, we would certainly lose time, and might have to stop on the way to the fire and beg a light. We can't afford to take any such chances as that. The engineer just grabs this torch and scratches it. The first bit of flame lights up the oil-soaked rags, and then he throws the whole thing into the fire box which is filled with pine shavings also soaked in oil, and there's the fire started. Then while he's traveling through the streets, he throws in whatever wood and coal are necessary and so he gets all the blaze that's needed before he has gone half a dozen blocks. Then you see that wrench hanging there beside the torch. Just before the engine gets to the hydrant they want to stop at, the engineer grabs that wrench, jumps off and runs ahead so as to have the hydrant open by the time the engine comes along. They attach the hydrant connection and then the tender comes up and passes them, leaving one end of the hose, and drives on until they have let out as many lengths as they want to use."

All this is done without any waste of time, for as I said to you before, there are no spare seconds in the New York fire service. Now come up stairs with me and I'll show you the sleeping quarters, which are somewhat similar to those around at our own place, except that they have three brass sliding poles instead of one, as we have. When the men are in bed, they have what they call a turnout on the floor beside them. Here is the turnout." He pointed, as he spoke, to a pair of trousers attached to a pair of rubber boots and so placed that they could be drawn on instantly.

"There's a gong here, too, you see, as well as down stairs, and when the alarm rings, the fireman jumps out of bed and, you might say, right into his turnout, pulls the trousers up and runs for the sliding pole, and there's a race every time to see who will get down first. The driver and engineer always sleep next to the poles so that they can get down ahead of the others. Down stairs there are two men on duty all the time at night. When the alarm sounds and the horses run to their places, these men must be at their heads to snap their collars and hitch the reins to their bits. The driver jumps into his seat, and the instant he sees that the harness is on all right, and that he has the number of the box from which the alarm has come, he starts away as fast as he can go. He doesn't wait to find out whether the engineer is there, or whether the other men have slid down the pole and are in their places—that's their business, not his. He has just one idea, and that is to get out into the street as soon as he can, and get to the fire before any other engine. The captain of the company rides on the ash-pan behind the engineer. His lieutenant rides with the driver of the tender, and the other men ride on the tender.

Just at this moment the gong rang sharply, and the horses, released from their stalls by the same electric current, sprang to their places in front of engine and hose carriage, and then a moment later trotted quietly back again.

"That's twelve o'clock that's just sounded," exclaimed Chief Trask, "and the horses always jump into their places every time the gong sounds. It wouldn't do to leave it to their judgment whether they should turn out or not, and besides, frequent alarms keep them from getting rusty. If they only turned out when there was a regular alarm, they would stay here sometimes two to three days at a time and that wouldn't be good for men or horses either. It's only by constant practice that we can be

kept always on the alert. You know that at
sea they often ring a false fire alarm, just for
the sake of keeping the ship's fire brigade in
practice. Now Captain Murphy will show you
the tender, or hose wagon as they used to call it."

Accordingly the captain showed Bruce the
two great coils of hose, and the different nozzles
fitted for different emergencies, and he told him
how the hook and ladder truck served at a fire
very much in the same capacity as the sapper
and miner corps in the army.

"The hook and ladder company carries the
picks and axes, scaling ladders, net and all that
sort of thing, while all we do is to turn a stream
of water on and put the fire out. There's a
good deal of competition between the different
companies and there's nothing we hate more
than to get to a fire and find that another company has got its stream on first. A few years
ago, when the Duke of Sutherland was here,
the fire commissioners determined to show him
what the New York department could do in
the way of getting to a fire in quick time. You
see, the Duke used to belong to the London
brigade, and has been what we call a 'fire crank'
all his life. They came down to this engine
house one night, and when they went away we
knew that the chances were that we'd be called

out before long. As they went up the street I heard the commissioner say to the Duke 'We'll go over to Twelfth street and Fifth avenue and ring the alarm there.' So I determined to have my men all ready so that at the very first stroke of the gong we could get out without waiting to get the number of the station. I made up my mind that I wasn't going to be beaten by any other company that night, so I had everything ready with the driver in his seat, and before the gong had struck twice, we were off. And we made such time getting over there, that we came up to where the party was standing and found the Duke with his hands still on the alarm box. You never saw a man more astonished in your life than he was."

On their way back the chief again impressed upon the boy's mind the enormous value of time. "It is necessary," he said, "first of all, to have everything in apple-pie order and ready to start at a moment's notice. Then when the alarm comes we must be ready and able to go without a second's delay. Each man has his own place to fill and if a man neglects to snap a horse's collar or the engineer fails to get to his place on the ash-pan in time, the chief of the battalion knows whom to blame."

CHAPTER IV.

ONE bright afternoon in May, Bruce found himself riding beside the chief up Fifth avenue, and as they rode the elder pointed out to him the principal public buildings, gave brief histories of some of the well known landmarks and explained how the great fortunes had been rolled up which enabled some men to live in Fifth avenue palaces with practically unlimited incomes.

Bruce wondered how it was that his guide should happen to know so much about the fashionable part of the city, even more in fact than he seemed to know about the poorer quarters. It may have been that Chief Trask saw what was uppermost in the boy's mind, for he said, as if in answer to a question, "I have to know about every part of the city, and it is particularly valuable for me to keep the run of what we call the brown stone district. The men who live here own property all over the city—factories, apartment houses, tenement houses and private dwellings—besides what they live in themselves. If there is ever a riot in the city, and I hope there will never be another one, the mob will make a rush for Fifth avenue. There are the Vanderbilt houses, those big brown buildings opposite the Cathedral. If fire were to consume them it would be a loss to the whole city, because they've got pictures and statues and books in them that could never be replaced. And my idea is that in time those valuable things will find their way into the Metropolitan Museum or some other public institution where they will be safe from fire and thieves, and can be seen by everybody."

Do they often have fires in these big brown stone houses?" asked Bruce.

"Not very often," replied Mr. Trask, "but they have them sometimes in the hotels and fashionable apartment houses, and perfect death traps some of those places are. There was one fire in a dwelling-house not long ago that came near proving fatal, and would have if it hadn't been for our hook and ladder company getting there in time. It wasn't much of a fire either, just what you might call a little blaze and a good deal of smoke in the third story, but it came near costing a lady her life all the same."

"How was that?" inquired the boy eagerly.

"Well" said the Chief, "it happened this way. The alarm came in one afternoon and of course we got right out. Probably if the alarm had told us that it was nothing but a little blaze in an upper room, we wouldn't have thought so much about getting there quickly, but luckily for all concerned, we got away just as quick as possible, and when we turned the corner into the street the first thing we saw was a big crowd of people dancing around and shouting to a lady who was sitting on a little narrow ledge right under the third story window of her house. The smoke was pouring out of the window just over her head, and she had to sit there crouched down so as to keep from being suffocated. Some of the people were crying but most of them were hollering to her, and most of those who were hollering were telling her to jump. She knew too much for them though, and just sat there as cool and patient as you please, waiting for us to come along and save her. As soon as we could get some of the people out of the way we had a ladder put up against the house and Charley Weyman started up it. As his foot touched the lower rung I saw that the woman was beginning to sway. The excitement and the smoke and all had been too much for her.

Charley made the best time he could to the top of the ladder, and caught her just as she toppled over. At that moment the window curtains took fire and swung out over her head in a blaze. I really think if we had been four seconds later than we were she would have lost her grip and fallen headlong to the street."

"Did Mr. Weyman carry her down the ladder in his arms?" inquired Bruce excitedly.

He carried her down about half-way and then she suddenly braced up, got out of his grasp, and came down the rest of the way herself. It was one of the narrowest escapes I have ever seen. And the lesson that it teaches a fireman is to be always ready for any emergency, and always on time to the half second. Seconds are like weeks in fighting fire."

For a few moments the two rode along in silence, and then the chief said "I'm going to take you up to headquarters to-day to give you an idea of how the telegraphic part of the service is conducted. The building we are going to is one of the most important in the whole city, and it would be a terrible thing for property owners if it were to be suddenly destroyed." As he said this he turned off into 67th street, and very soon drew up in front of what looked like an engine house with four or five extra stories added to it. Leaving the horse in a covered court-yard beside the tall building, they made their way to the upper floor in which was the elaborate, costly and ingenious telegraphic apparatus employed exclusively by the fire depatment.

As they entered, a telegraphic operator arose from his desk and came forward to greet them. Chief Trask shook him by the hand, and told him that he had brought the boy up there in order to begin his education in the duties of a fireman.

"That's good" replied the operator, "and it's a good thing to begin here for this is what you might call the heart of the whole system. If this part were to stop working, all the rest of it would be paralyzed."

While he was speaking, the tick of a telegraph instrument was heard, and the operator immediately turned away.

"That's an alarm from box 323," said the chief in a low voice, for he had listened to the ticking too. "Now you'll see him send a dispatch to the companies which are to go out. He sends two dispatches. One to ring the little gong in each engine house, and the other, which acts as a check on the first, to ring on the big gong. The first he sends by means of a switch and the second by that machine over there in a glass case. That one acts automatically."

By this time the operator, having notified the different companies situated in the vicinity of the fire, returned and expressed his willingness to explain the whole system to the young boy. For fully half an hour they remained in the operating room where Bruce saw the careful and systematic manner in which every fire is recorded—they average about ten a day—while by means of a peculiar apparatus on the wall the operator can tell exactly what engine companies are out on duty, and what ones are in their quarters ready to respond to an alarm. In this way he knows what to do in the event of two fires in the same vicinity.

As they were taking their leave Chief Trask stopped in a large room fitted up with various gymnastic appliances: "This," he said, "is the gymnasium used by the men who wish positions in the department. They come here and practice, and then when the Board sits to determine on their application they show what they can do on the rings, the horizontal bar and the ladder, the same as if they were giving an exhibition at an athletic club. My idea has always been" he continued, as they walked down stairs "to have a special training school the same as they have for the Navy, in which boys can be taught to become firemen. Our great trouble is that the men don't begin this exercising and gymnastics until they're of age, and it's very hard for them to acquire activity and quickness. I think boys could be brought up with special reference to entering the fire department, and taught to do all sorts of tricks such as climbing ladders and making high jumps."

"Oh! I was always good at climbing and things like that," responded Bruce, "and up in the country there wasn't a boy anywhere around who could go up a walnut tree quicker than I could, or who dared go as far out on a branch as I would. You'll find me all right in that part of the business as soon as you give me a show."

"I'm glad to hear that," rejoined the chief, "and it won't be long before I'll give you a chance to see what you can do."

His few words had a wonderful effect on Bruce Decker. He had not yet dared to whisper to the chief the hope which he had cherished that he would soon be allowed to go out on the truck and assist in putting out a fire, and now it seemed to him that the moment was at hand when he was to have his long sought for chance to distinguish himself. He was in a merry mood that night as he bedded down the horses and washed the Chief's wagon. How soon would he become a member of the department? How soon would he rise to become Chief of a Battalion?

CHAPTER V.

ONE morning Bruce Decker stood leaning on the chain stretched across the entrance to the quarters, wondering how soon he would be allowed to go to fires with the men. Ever since his arrival in New York it had been his highest ambition to climb up on the truck when the alarm sounded, and be off to the scene of action. But much as he desired to bear his share in the work of the company, he had never dared broach the subject to his superiors. To begin with, the rigid discipline of the department and the unhesitating, unquestioning way in which the men obeyed the orders of their superiors, had made a deep impression on the young country boy, and besides, he was eager to have them all believe that he was a sober, cool-headed, trustworthy person rather than a flighty boy, carried away with the idea of an exciting and adventurous fireman's life.

The company went out on an average about twice a day, and while the men were away Bruce remained in the quarters, sometimes engaged in some light work about the place, and sometimes reading or studying. He was always on hand to help bed down the horses on their return, and to find out from the men where the fire had been. Sometimes the company returned in less than an hour, sometimes they were gone more than two hours, and once they had remained out all night, while Bruce sat by the open door wondering fearfully what had become of them.

To-day, as he stood leaning on the iron chain, he determined to ask from the chief permission to go out at the next alarm, and he had just reached this conclusion when his thoughts were interrupted by the familiar voice of his superior.

"Bruce," said the chief, "I want you to take this letter up to Mr. Dewsnap on Madison avenue, and get an answer to it. Be sure you see him, and if he is not at home, wait till he does come in."

Glad of an excuse to get out into the streets, for it was a pleasant warm day, Bruce bent his steps towards the address indicated on the envelope which he carried in his hand. A man servant answered his ring and ushered him into the large and rather gloomy library, in which sat Mr. Peter Dewsnap, one of the eccentric characters of New York, and a particular friend of Chief Trask's. Mr. Dewsnap was a short and rather stout gentleman, with bright, clear eyes, snow-white whiskers and a decidedly jovial aspect. He smiled pleasantly as he took the letter, and then asked the boy to sit down, remarking at the same time, "You're not one of the chief's sons are you?"

"No, sir," replied Bruce, rather proudly, "I'm a member of his company."

"A member of the fire company!" exclaimed Mr. Dewsnap, "Well, you must have joined very lately, and in fact I didn't know that there were any lads as young as you in the whole department."

"I've only been there a very short time, sir," replied the boy, respectfully, "but my father was a member of this company until his death, about four months ago."

"You don't mean to say that you are a son of Frank Decker, who was killed at that big apartment house fire?" cried Mr. Dewsnap, and then added, as he scanned the boy's face more carefully, "yes, the same eyes and the same square look in them. I knew your father very well, young man, and I'm glad to see you. Did you never hear your father speak of me?"

And just then a sudden remembrance of what his father had told him lit up the boy's mind, and he exclaimed hastily, and without thinking of what he was saying: "Why, you're not the gentleman they used to call the old fire crank, are you?"

He stopped suddenly, as soon as the words were out of his mouth, realizing that he had addressed the old gentleman in a too familiar way. But the latter did not seem to be offended. On the contrary, he threw himself back in his chair, uttering roars of laughter and slapping his knees with his hand: "That's what I am, and that's just what your father used to call me," he cried, "I'm an old fire crank, and have been ever since I was your age, and that's fifty years ago. There was no paid department then, with all its new fangled inventions for getting out in less than no time, but we had a volunteer department, and I belonged to it. You boys of the present generation can't form any idea of what New York was like when I was your age. You've not been in the city long, have you?"

"No, sir, replied Bruce simply, "I was brought up in the country, and never saw New York until a fortnight ago."

I thought I saw some of the country tan on your face," rejoined the old gentleman. "Well, you see how thick the houses are around here on Madison avenue near Fortieth street, this is about where I used to pick blackberries when I was a lad. The city was a good ways off then, and they used to ring a big bell when there was a fire. Some of the best men in the town were firemen, and some of the toughest citizens as well. They had nothing but hand engines then, but there was just as sharp a race to get to the fire and get a stream on in those days as there is to-day. And many's the fight I've seen between the rival companies. They used to call us toughs and rowdies, but there wasn't so much of that after the Fire Zouaves were recruited and sent to the front in the early days of the war. They showed then, that their experience in fignting had taught them something that was of some use to their country, and there were no such soldiers, either on our side or with the Confederates, as the boys in the red trousers and gaiters that went South with Ellsworth and Duryea. However, I can talk all night when I get started on that subject. Some afternoon I'll have Chief Trask bring you up here and I'll show you some old souvenirs of the volunteer department that I've got, and tell you some stories of Big Six and the Black Joke, and half a dozen more of the famous old-time organizations. Since I retired from business ten years ago, I've become more of a fire crank, as they call it, than I was before the war. By the way, if the chief is down at the quarters now, I'll step down and see him."

"He was there when I left," said Bruce, "and told me to bring him an answer to his letter."

"Very well, you can bring me down there as an answer," said the jolly old gentleman, as he put on his hat, took his gold-headed cane from behind the door and ushered his young guest into the hall with punctilious, old-fashioned courtesy. They walked together down the broad avenue, Mr. Dewsnap pausing occasionally to point out to his young companion some building of historic interest, or the scene of some great conflagration. They had just reached the Fifth Avenue Hotel, and Mr. Dewsnap was telling Bruce about the circus which used to occupy the present site of the house, when a sharp clang of a gong fell upon their ears, and they saw Captain Murphy's steam engine thundering along Twenty-third street, while Chief Trask in his wagon came up Broadway at full gallop, closely followed by the hook and ladder truck, with Charlie Weyman in the driver's seat, Brophy at the tiller, and the men, some of whom were still struggling with their coats, clinging to the truck as best they could.

In an instant the old gentleman's face changed, and his eyes seemed to blaze with excitement.

"Come with me!" he exclaimed, as he darted after the flying vehicles. Up Broadway he went, with Bruce in swift pursuit, then turning into Twenty-fifth street, he followed on to Sixth avenue, arriving just as Captain Murphy had his hose attached to the hydrant and was ready to throw a stream wherever it might be needed. A crowd had collected in front of a building from whose upper window a volume of smoke issued. Chief Trask was standing on the sidewalk giving order to his men, and just as they appeared on the scene, one of the men from the engine company entered the hallway with a nozzle of the hose in his hand and disappeared upstairs, while a ladder from the truck was placed against the side of the building, and a fireman ran hastily up to see that there were no people imprisoned in the upper story.

But the fire proved a very slight one, and within a very few minutes the smoke had ceased to issue from the upper window, the hose had been replaced in the tender and the long ladder on the truck. And it was just at this moment that Chief Trask recognized Mr. Dewsnap and came forward, holding out his hand and saying: "I just sent a note up to your house, and you'll probably find it there when you get back. If I'd known we were to get a call from this box, I wouldn't have sent it, but would have taken my chances of seeing you here. You very seldom miss a fire that's anywhere within your radius."

I got your note, and was just going down with that boy of yours to see you, when we met you coming up," rejoined the old gentleman, "and so we concluded we'd follow you along and take in the fire, too. I'm very much obliged to you for your kind offer, and you may expect to see me with those gentlemen within a few days. I've told them both about the way we do things in the New York department, but I don't think they believe it. Now I want to prove it to them, because I am getting rather tired of the way some of these foreigners pretend to look down on us Americans."

"Very well," rejoined Chief Trask, "bring them down any time you feel like it, and you'll find us ready. You needn't take the trouble to notify me when you're coming, except that I'd like to be there myself. If my men don't get the truck out into the street in ten seconds, I want to know the reason why every time."

"I want you to come up and call on me some afternoon," said Mr. Dewsnap to Bruce, as the boy turned to go back with the men on the truck. "I've got a number of books relating to the fire department and some curiosities that ought to interest a boy of your age and inclinations. You'll find me at home any afternoon between two and four, and I'm sure Chief Trask will give you permission to come."

Then, with a pleasant smile and nod, the old gentleman climbed into the chief's wagon, while Bruce scrambled up over the wheel of the big truck and rolled slowly back to quarters.

Chapter VI.

BRUCE had always been fond of reading since his earliest childhood, and it was his habit, when not otherwise employed, to spend most of his time seated in the back room of the quarters reading whatever books or newspapers he could find there. These books and newspapers were contributed by different well-disposed people who, having more reading matter than they required, remembered the firemen, and distributed them along the different engine houses in the town. One morning, while the boy was engaged in this manner, a tall, well-built and military looking gentleman, who seemed to be fully seventy years of age, entered the quarters and inquired for the chief.

"He's upstairs, sir, but I'll call him down," said Bruce, promptly rising and offering the old gentleman a chair. Then he went upstairs and a moment later the chief came down and quickly recognized in his visitor an acquaintance known as Mr. Samuel Dexter, who lived in an old-fashioned house in the northern part of the city.

Mr. Dexter told him that he had called simply to gratify his curiosity in regard to the fire department, and after the chief had shown him the different sorts of apparatus kept there, and explained the method of getting out quickly, his visitor asked him what they did for reading matter.

"Well, we are dependent on our friends for that," replied the chief, "there are a number of people who send us books and papers from time to time, and without them, I can assure you that the hours would hang pretty heavily on our hands."

"Why, I have a lot of books and magazines in my garret that I shall never have any use for," exclaimed Mr. Dexter, "and if you could send up for them some day, I would be very glad to let you have them." Chief Trask thanked him for his offer and turning to Bruce who stood by, directed him to drive up there in one of his wagons the next morning and get the periodicals.

The next day accordingly, Bruce started in the chief's wagon and drove slowly up Lexington avenue, then turning to the right and crossing the Harlem river he found himself in an entirely strange part of the city. There were not many houses to be seen, and down near the water were great stretches of open fields and in some places heaps of lumber and enormous bins of coal. Continuing in a northerly direction he soon found the quiet avenue on which Mr. Dexter lived, and then he entered a wide gate and drove along a short roadway leading to a big, square, gloomy looking stone house, completely hidden from the street by a dense hedge and some thick clusters of fir trees.

He knew from the description that had been given him that he had found the right place, and somehow, the house, the big hedge and the front doorway seemed strangely familiar to him. It seemed to him that some time in the remote past he had either been there before or else dreamt of just such a place, only the picture that had remained faintly outlined in his mind was of a house and hedge and trees that were fully five times as tall as those which he now saw before him. And then it seemed to him that the old picture which had lingered, though forgotten, in his mind for so many years contained also another door in the same house, a side door that was smaller and shaded by vines that clambered about a wooden porch. He had alighted from the wagon by this time and, impelled by curiosity, he tied his horse to a post in which was set a great rusty iron ring,

"For fully a minute Bruce stood looking at the house."
Page 47.

and then walked around the house to see if his dream or memory whatever it might be, would prove true.

Yes, there was the old doorway with the clematis clambering about it, just as his fancy had painted it, except that the door seemed smaller, and the clinging vines less luxuriant than in his dream. For fully a minute Bruce stood looking at the house and wondering when he could have seen it before, or whether it was simply an accidental freak of his imagination that made the scene seem so familiar to him.

He was still looking and wondering when the door opened and Mr. Dexter himself appeared on the doorsill.

"Come in young man," he said, "you've come up for those old books and magazines I suppose."

"Yes sir," replied the boy, taking off his hat respectfully. "Chief Trask sent me up for them with the wagon. Following the old gentleman, he entered a dark hallway, in one corner of which stood a heap of novels, books of travel, magazines and other publications, which had been brought down that morning from the garret. The boy's eyes glistened as he looked at the big heap, and thought of the pleasure that he would have in going through them, during his next leisure hours. Aided by one of Mr. Dexter's servants, he placed them in the wagon, and then, having thanked the old gentleman for his kindness, he drove slowly down the winding roadway, and thence through the gate into the street. He stopped a moment to look at the landscape that lay stretched before him, hoping that he might see in it some object that, like the old front porch would recall some childish memory, but there was nothing that was in any way familiar to him, and he drove away shaking his head and very much puzzled by what he had seen. He was still thinking over the events of the day and wondering whether he had ever seen Mr. Dexter before, for his face too had a familiar look and somehow seemed to be perfectly in accord with the old stone house and the big, solemn hedge that hid it from the road, when his attention was attracted by a voice that seemed to come almost from under the carriage wheels.

"I say, can't you give me a lift? I've hurt my ankle," was what he heard, as he hastily pulled up his horse and there, seated on a big rock, by the roadside, was a young boy, apparently not more than fifteen years of age, whose handsome clothes were torn and dust-covered, and whose face was deathly pale. Bruce alighted at once from the wagon and asked him what the matter was.

"I was just on my way home," replied the boy, "and I tried to make a running jump over those rocks, when I slipped and fell, now it hurts me to touch my foot to the ground, and my left ankle hurts me awfully. Can't you take me home in your wagon? My father will pay you for your trouble."

"Certainly, I'll give you a lift," replied Bruce, "but your father needn't pay me anything for it; just stand up beside me and I'll lift you in."

With a little trouble, he placed the boy in the seat and then climbed in himself and sat down beside him. The two lads were not slow in making one another's acquaintance. The injured boy said that his name was Harry Van Kuren and he pointed out his father's house, a large handsome residence surrounded by well kept grounds. He was fifteen years old, he said, and did not go to school, but had a private tutor who lived in the house with him, and nearly always accompanied him when he went out to walk or ride.

"And how do you happen to be here?" inquired young Van Kuren.

Then Bruce told him of his errand to Mr. Dexter's and showed him the pile of books and magazines which he was taking back for the firemen to read.

"But you don't mean to say that you belong to the fire department, do you?" exclaimed Harry excitedly.

"Yes, I've been on the force pretty near three months," answered Bruce proudly.

"My, but you're a lucky chap," cried his companion. "I just wish my father would let me join, but he won't let me do anything I want to. I never have any fun anyway; there's nothing to do in this stupid old place, except to go riding on my pony, and once in a while have a sail on the Sound. There are no other boys for me to play with—that is, none that I like—and I have to go in the house every night at six and stay there till bedtime. I suppose you have all the fun in the world getting up in the middle of the night and going to fires, and driving like mad through the streets. Say, why can't you let me go out with you some time.

But Bruce shook his head dubiously, he was willing to have the boy imagine that he himself was one of the leading members of the company, and he wished moreover to impress him with the idea that it was no easy matter for a young boy to become a member of the New York Fire Department. "I'm afraid," he said, "that you'd find it very difficult to get an appointment. I believe I'm the youngest member of the whole department, and I know I never would have been taken on, if it hadn't been on account of my father, who was a fireman before me."

"And is your father on the department yet?" demanded Harry.

"No," replied Bruce with a little choking sound in his voice, "he was killed at a fire some months ago and then they gave me a position on account of him."

"Your father was killed at a fire? Oh I'm awfully sorry!" exclaimed Harry! "who was an impulsive and warm-hearted, although somewhat spoiled boy, "but I'm going to tell my father about you, and ask him if you can't come up and visit me some time. Here's our entrance; just drive me down to the side door will you please, and I'll get one of the servants to help me up stairs."

Bruce helped his new friend to alight and then a man servant appeared in answer to his ring, and on learning that his young master was hurt, started off in much alarm in quest of the private tutor, but was called back imperiously by young Master Harry and ordered to "lend a hand" in getting him into the house.

As Bruce turned to leave, the boy held out his hand in a frank, straightforward way that was very agreeable and said, "I'm very much obliged to you for bringing me home, and now that I've got your address I'm going to write and ask you to come up and see me. My father will be mad enough when he comes home and finds what's happened to me, because he told me I wasn't to go off the grounds to-day. But he'll come around all right in a week then we'll have fun together."

And as Bruce drove out of the handsome grounds of Mr. Van Kuren's house, he felt that it had been a well spent and eventful day for him. He felt sure that he had made a friend in young Van Kuren, and then he fell to thinking of Mr. Dexter and his big stone house and his familiar looking porch and the little side door with its clinging vines, and he wondered for the hundredth time under what circumstances he could have seen them before.

Chapter VII.

WITH the possible exception of John Trask, it is doubtful if Bruce had a better friend in the whole company than Charley Weyman, who drove the truck and was looked upon as one of the nerviest and most active firemen in the battalion. Weyman had been Frank Decker's most intimate friend, and the natural interest which he took in the son was deepened by the readiness shown by the latter to oblige his new friend and to help him in every possible way in the discharge of his duty.

It was not unnatural then that Bruce should decide to repeat to Weyman his strange experiences at Mr. Dexter's house, and accordingly one afternoon, a few days subsequent to his visit, he said to the fireman, just as they had seated themselves for a quiet game of checkers: "There was a funny thing happened to me the other day when I went after those books, and I'd like to know if you could give me any explanation of it."

"Well, what was the funny thing?" inquired the other, as he moved one of his men in the direction of the king row.

"Well, you know Chief Trask sent me up to Mr. Dexter's house to get a lot of books and magazines. I don't suppose you were ever up there, were you?"

"No, can't say that I ever was, but it's your move," rejoined Weyman.

"It's a great big house," went on Bruce, as he moved one of his men so carelessly that his opponent instantly took it, "in fact it's one of the finest houses I was ever in. There's a big, thick hedge that separates it from the street, and when you get inside the hedge there's a roadway that winds through a big, thick clump of firs and pines, right up to the front door of the house. The minute I came inside the gate the place took on a familiar look and I was positive that some time or other I'd been there before. When I stopped in front of the door, that looked familiar too, and then I seemed to remember that there was another door on the other side of the house that was smaller and had a little porch over it, so as to shade the doorstep. Just to see if I was right or not, I got out and walked around the house and there, sure enough, was the side door, just as I had either dreamt it or remembered it some time ever so many years ago; only it seemed to me that in reality the place was only about one quarter as big as I had imagined it."

By this time Weyman had become so much interested in the boy's narrative that he had ceased entirely to think of the game and was now gazing at Bruce in the intense manner of one who is hearing some startling piece of news in which he has a strong personal interest.

"You say that you remember the place and yet you were never there before?" demanded the fireman.

"Yes," answered the boy, "and moreover I don't think that I could have seen a picture of it, for the smell of the flowers and of the vines over the porch was just as familiar to my nostrils as the doorway was to my eyes. I don't think I could ever have been there before, and it seemed to me as if I had dreamt of the place, not once, but a great many times."

For a moment or two Charles Weyman was silent, then he pushed away the checkerboard and said: "What you've just told me, Bruce, is very curious and seems to confirm an idea that came to me long ago when your father was alive. Do you know anything about your father or his relations?"

Bruce thought a minute, and then answered:
"No, I never knew he had any relations. I was

brought up by some old people who lived in the country on the shore of Lake Ontario and only saw my father once a year. Then he never used to talk to me about anything except the fire company, and it was that that made me crazy to join the service. If he had any brothers or sisters or cousins he never mentioned them to me, and to tell the truth this is the first time in my life that I ever thought about the subject."

"But didn't your mother have any relations who are living now?" inquired Weyman.

"Not that I ever heard of. She died when I was very young and I can scarcely remember her. Since then I lived with those old people, who took care of me, but after my father died, I determined to strike out for myself and so I came down to New York."

"Well, if I were you," said Weyman, "I would write home to someone in the country who knew your father, and make some inquiries about his family. In fact, I should think you'd like to know who you are. There was always something mysterious about your father —something that I never could understand. He was a man of much better education than any of the rest of us, and I remember once or twice seeing well dressed gentlemen, evidently men of high position, stop in the streets to shake hands and talk with him. On such occasions he never offered any explanation except to ask me not to speak of it to the other men. Well as I knew him, I never knew positively that he had a child living, and I was more surprised than any man in the company when you turned up that afternoon and told us you were Frank Decker's son."

"But," exclaimed Bruce, who, of course, had become very much interested in his companion's words, "didn't you ever hear him say anything or mention any name that could serve as a sort of clue to his origin? If I had anything to work on, I might follow it up and perhaps find out who his relations were. However, perhaps it would not be worth the trouble, for they might not be particularly glad to have a poor boy like me, who hasn't a cent in the world, turn up and claim connection with them. I think I am just about as well off here as I would be with any of my kin."

"There are one or two things about your father that come to my mind now," said Weyman, after a moment's reflection, "and although I gave them no thought at the time, still they might be of some use to you. There was a man who came around to see him once in a while, and when he came the two always went out and walked up and down the street, talking together. Sometimes they got excited, and I noticed that your father was never the same after one of these visits. He would sit in a corner, moody and sullen, sometimes talking to himself, and it would take him a couple of days to get back to his old frame of mind again. He was naturally a light-hearted, jovial fellow, and that's why I couldn't help noticing the effect these visits had on him."

"What sort of a looking man was he, who called on him, and always seemed to upset him so?" asked the boy.

"He was tall and dark and well-dressed, and I'd know him anywhere by a scar he had on his face that was partly hidden by a stiff black beard he always wore. The last time he was here was the day before the big fire at which your father was killed. I remember it well, because that morning before the first alarm came in Frank hardly spoke to me, but sat over there in that corner, smoking his pipe and looking as if he had lost the last friend he had on earth."

"And you don't know who that dark man was or what name he gave?" said the boy.

Weyman shook his head slowly. "No," he said, "I did know his name once, but it passed out of my mind. If I were you, I would write a letter up to the country and see if I couldn't find out something in the way of a clue."

Just at this moment Chief Trask came in and told Bruce to hitch up the wagon and go with him up to headquarters, and so the conversation came to an end. But all that day the young boy was very thoughtful, and when night came he had determined to set to work, quietly and persistently, to find out something about his father and his mother, and to learn if he had any kindred living in the world. He had no clues to follow except the legend of the dark man with the scar on his face, and the resemblance of Philip Dexter's house to something of which he had once dreamt and still had a vague recollection.

Chapter VIII.

FOR fully a fortnight after his strange experience in the upper part of the city, Bruce heard nothing from Harry Van Kuren, the boy whom he had picked up by the roadside and conveyed home. He had hoped, at first, that their chance acquaintance might develop into a permanent friendship, for since his arrival in the city he had associated entirely with the men in the fire company and, boy like, he was beginning to pine for the companionship of lads of his own age. Two or three times he had thought of writing a note to Harry to ask him how his foot was getting along, but he had hesitated, for fear he should be looked upon as endeavoring to intrude upon a boy whose condition in life was, he could not help feeling, very much better than his own. So Bruce, who was an independent, self-respecting lad, determined to let the other make the first advance, if he desired to continue the acquaintance.

One morning, however, about a fortnight after the first meeting of the two boys, Bruce was surprised and delighted to see Harry march into the quarters and come straight up to where he was sitting.

"I suppose you thought I was never coming down here to see you," said the visitor as he shook Bruce heartily by the hand, "but the fact is when my father got home that night and found that I had been out without his leave, he put me on bounds for two weeks and said if he caught me going out without permission he would lock me up in the house. I was going to write to you, but writing is an awful bother, so I thought I'd wait until I got off the limit and then come down here and make you a call."

Bruce was heartily glad to see his visitor, and frankly told him so, mentioning also the fact that he had almost given up hope of hearing from him again.

"Oh I never forget my friends," said Harry "and here's a letter from my father inviting you come up and spend the afternoon with us to-day."

With these words he produced from the inside pocket of his jacket a polite and formal letter addressed to Bruce Decker, Esq., and signed "Horace Van Kuren," in which the writer hoped that Mr. Decker would honor him with his company at dinner that evening, in order that he might thank him for the kindness shown to his son some time before.

Bruce felt staggered at the idea of dining in that great, beautiful house, and at first did not know what reply to make ; then he bethought him of Charley Weyman and accordingly went up stairs and submitted the letter to him. The latter read it carefully and then said : "You had better go by all means, it's a good chance for you to get acquainted with those people and they can't do you any harm."

"But" said the boy in a diffident, hesitating way, "I'm almost afraid to go up there because I haven't got any clothes nice enough. This is the best suit I've got, and that boy Harry is togged out in beautiful things, and I feel ashamed to go along with him, because of the contrast between us.

"Nonsense! he wasn't ashamed to ride in the chief's wagon the other day, was he?"

"Why no," replied the boy, "I never thought of it then, and I don't think he did either. Anyway he didn't say anything about it, and now he's come down to see me, and his father has asked me up to visit them.

"You'd better go with him," said the fireman, "and my opinion is that they'll take you just as you are. Anyway, you can tell by the way they treat you, particularly by the way this boy treats you, whether they are the right sort of people or not."

Bruce accordingly went to Chief Trask, showed him the letter, and asked his permission to go with the boy, and having received it—and it was granted all the more willingly because he was always obedient and industrious himself, and seldom asked any favors,—he carefully washed his hands and face, brushed his clothes and shoes and made ready to start.

Meantime Harry had been examining everything in the building with much interest, and he now called to the other boy to explain to him how the alarms came in, and how the men got off to the fire when they heard the gong. All this was now an old story to the young fire boy who had so familiarized himself with every detail that he was able to give his new friend a complete and graphic description of the workings of the system.

Harry wanted to stay until an alarm was sent in so that he might see the company start, but when he found that it might be necessary to wait two days for a fire to occur in their district he gave the plan up, and they started off together. Bruce was relieved to see that in spite of his fine clothes, and generally stylish appearance young Van Kuren treated him with as much courtesy as it is possible for one boy to show to another and, so far from making any remarks about their difference in dress, did not seem to notice what sort of a coat his companion wore. As a matter of fact, Harry did notice the coat with its rather shabby sleeves and a good many other little things, for he was a quick-witted observant boy, but he was too well bred to make any remarks on the subject. Indeed it would be hard to find anywhere a boy of better breeding than this spoiled, willful, impulsive child of luxury, who was always getting into trouble of one sort or another, was always doing thoughtless and foolish things, and yet was liked by every one who knew him. When he noticed Bruce's coat, it suggested to him, not the idea of making fun of it, but the wish that he could get him another without hurting his feelings.

Both boys were in high spirits as they trudged along, the one because he had at last found a companion of his own age, the other because he saw a chance to mingle on familiar terms with the men of the fire department, and perhaps to even ride to a fire on the truck with the rest of the company. The New York boy of to-day knows no higher ambition than to join the fire department and ride to fires on the swift rolling engine, and Harry Van Kuren was a New York boy through and through.

"Watch me scare that Dutchman!" he cried as they drew near a basement beer saloon, at the door of which a corpulent German was peacefully dozing. A pile of kegs stood on the top of a short flight of steps, and with a warning cry of "Look out Dutchy!" Harry toppled the heap over and then seizing his comrade by the hand ran for dear life. The saloon keeper pursued them for a few yards and then gave up the chase, while Harry much elated by his exploit looked around for some other victim for his practical humor.

Bruce, accustomed as he was to the rigid discipline maintained by Chief Trask, was horrified at his companion's idea of sport, and was glad enough when they reached the elevated station without any further adventures.

A little girl not more than thirteen years old, was standing by the front gate of Mr. Van Kuren's house when the two boys entered; she had blue eyes, a profusion of light hair, which she wore in a single braid down her back, and was altogether extremely pretty and attractive.

"You'll catch it when you get into the house," she remarked to Harry, with a knowing wag of her head.

"What for?" he demanded.

"For going off without letting Mr. Reed know."

"Oh, bother!" said the boy, "I forgot all about him. He's my tutor, you see," he added, turning to Bruce, "and this is my sister Laura."

Bruce took off his cap and bowed politely to the young girl, and she held out her hand and said, without any apparent reserve or shyness, "I saw you the other day when you brought Harry home; why didn't you drive up in your wagon to-day? it must be fun to be a firemen; I wish you'd tell me all about it. Harry, you'd better go in the house and see Mr. Reed right off; he's hopping mad, and if he don't get over it before papa comes back, you'll be locked up for another fortnight. Harry is always getting locked up," she continued, turning to the visitor, who was listening with considerable surprise to this frank conversation between the brother and sister.

Harry disappeared into the house, saying that he would be out as soon as he had "squared himself with the professor," and

Laura took Bruce off to show him the stable where her pony was, and the barns and sheds in which were kept cows, pigs, dogs, and even a pair of goats.

Chapter IX.

THE Van Kuren mansion and grounds constituted one of the finest places in the upper part of New York, and to Bruce, accustomed to plain ways of living, it seemed almost like some enchanted palace in fairyland. For fully an hour he strolled about the grounds under the guidance of Miss Laura Van Kuren, who talked to him as freely and frankly as if she had known him all her life. Harry was in disgrace, she said, for going off without consulting his tutor, and he would probably be kept in the house until he had learned and recited the lesson which had been given him that morning. Meantime she would entertain his guest herself, and as she was very pretty, very bright, and altogether very friendly and charming, Bruce did not feel the absence of her brother to any great extent. In fact, he was mean enough to hope in his secret heart that Mr. Reed would keep him in the house all the rest of the afternoon so that he and Laura might continue their confidential talk as they walked about together.

And as they talked, Bruce, who was naturally a diffident boy, became emboldened to such a degree that he made up his mind to ask the young girl if she knew anything about Mr. Dexter and the big, old fashioned house, which had seemed familiar ground to her. The opportunity for putting the question soon came. They were sitting together in a small summer house, eating some strawberries which they had picked in the garden, taking advantage of a moment when the gardener was off in another part of the grounds.

"Did you ever know a Mr. Dexter, who lives near here?" inquired Bruce, during a pause in the conversation.

The girl looked up quickly as she said, "You don't mean that old gentleman who lives over there about half a mile along the road, do you?"

"Yes, he lives in a big square stone house," said the boy.

Laura cast a hasty and apprehensive glance around her, and then said in lowered tones, as if she feared that some one were listening, "I know who he is, but papa won't let us go near his house. Papa says that he's a bad man and he won't have anything to do with him, but I think he's real nice, and one day, about a year ago, I was out walking near there, and he saw me and called me in and gave me some big bunches of splendid grapes, and then he asked me my name, and when I told him he seemed surprised, and somehow he wasn't nice any more, and in a minute or two he told me that I had better run home or my people would be anxious about me. When I got home I told papa about it, and he was awfully angry, and said that I must never go into that yard again, and that if I saw Mr. Dexter coming I must run away. I asked him why, and he wouldn't tell me. But where did you ever hear of him?"

Bruce hesitated a few minutes before replying, and then made answer, "The chief of our battalion, Mr. Trask, sent me up there the other day on an errand."

"And did you go inside the grounds and into the house?" demanded Laura, excitedly. "Do tell me all about it, for it is such a romantic looking place that I always feel as if there were some mysterious story connected with it. And then that old Mr. Dexter never goes out anywhere, and nobody seems to know anything about him. My nurse, the one who lived with us for twenty-five years, told me once that Mr. Dexter and papa used to be great friends, but they had some kind of a quarrel. I asked her what they quarreled about and she wouldn't tell me, although I am sure she knows all about it."

The young girl's words of course made a deep impression on Bruce, who was now more curious than ever to learn the history of the kindly old gentleman who lived all by himself in the big, square stone house behind the thick hedge.

"Go on and tell me all about what you saw there," said Laura eagerly. "I am sure there's some mystery about the place like the ones we read about in the story books. When I was a little bit of a girl, I used to imagine there was a sleeping beauty hidden away behind those dark trees and I expected that some day a prince would come and wake her up and that then there'd be a grand party for everybody around here to go to."

"Well, there is a mystery about it, and it's one I'd like very much to solve," said Bruce quietly.

"A mystery!" exclaimed Laura, "Now you must tell me everything about it before you leave this summer-house," and she spoke in the tones of a young girl who expected to have her own way.

"I don't know whether I ought to say anything to you about it or not," began the boy in a doubtful voice, "and besides you might not be interested in the mystery because after all it only concerns myself."

"Go right on and tell me this very minute!" cried the girl imperiously.

"You'll promise never to tell as long as you live and breathe?"

"Hope to die, if I do," rejoined Laura fervently, "Now, go on."

Thus adjured, Bruce told her the story of his visit to Mr. Dexter's house and the strangely familiar look that the place had worn; and he told her, too, of the conversation that he had had with Charley Weyman and of the advice that the latter had given him. Laura listened to his words with the deepest attention, and when he had finished, she drew a long breath and said "that's the most interesting, romantic thing I ever heard about in all my life. And you don't really know who your folks are? Why you might be almost anybody in the world, and may be you're the prince who will come and waken up the princess with a kiss, the same as in the story book. But how are you going to work to find out what it all means? You must tell me everything you do about it

Bruce tells Laura the story of his visit to Mr. Dexter's house.--
Page 72.

for I'll never be able to sleep at night until you're restored to your rights."

Bruce, who was of a rather practical turn of mind, was amused at the excitement of his more imaginative companion. Up to this moment he had simply felt a curiosity to learn why it was that the Dexter homestead seemed familiar to him, and it had never occurred to him that he had any particular "rights" to be restored to him, or that any grave question depended on the fancied resemblance of the place to the one pictured in his memory.

"I would like very much to learn something about Mr. Dexter and his old house, but I don't know how to go about it. I always lived in the country, and, outside the men in our fire company, I have no friends or even acquaintances in New York. You have lived here all your life, and everything seems natural to you, but you've no idea what a big, lonely, desolate place this city is to a boy like me who comes here as a stranger.

"I'll tell you what," exclaimed Laura suddenly, "when my papa comes home to-night—you know you're going to stay to dinner with us—you ask him about Mr. Dexter but don't tell him that you said a word to me about it. Maybe he'll tell you something that will be of some use to you, but don't say a word to him about what you told me about your visit there. We must keep that for our own secret, and I shall be mad if you tell him or Harry or anybody else, and if I get mad I won't help you to find out the mystery of it. Now, you must do just what I tell you or else I won't like you any more."

"What secret are you talking about?" demanded some one close beside them in a voice so loud that both Laura and Bruce started in surprise from their seats. It was Harry who had just been released by his tutor and had been, according to his own account, hunting them all over the grounds.

Laura put her finger on her lips and threw a significant glance at Bruce, and so it happened that Harry learned nothing of what they had been talking about for fully half an hour.

At six o'clock, Mr. Van Kuren reached home. He shook hands with Bruce and told him he was glad to see him and thanked him for his kindness to Harry.

Bruce noticed that both children appeared to stand in wholesome awe of their parent, obeying him with the utmost alacrity and conversing only in low tones while he was present. This was not surprising to the young visitor, for Mr. Van Kuren impressed him as a stern, silent, self-contained man, who might be very severe if he chose to. But his face was not unkind, and in the few remarks that he addressed to his guest he showed a certain interest in his welfare and a desire to make him feel as much at home as it was possible for a shy, country boy, unaccustomed to the ways of society, to feel in a splendid house like the one in which he found himself now. But all idea of asking him about the Dexter mansion left his mind, and although he found himself alone with him for a few moments before dinner was announced, he simply did not dare to broach the subject that was uppermost in his mind.

The dinner to which he sat down seemed to Bruce a very grand affair. It was served in a large, square room, wainscoated in dark wood and furnished in a rich, simple and tasteful fashion. The round table was covered with a white damask cloth of beautiful texture and the glass and silver seemed to have been polished with wonderful care. Colored wax candles with silk shades shed a soft light. Besides Mr. Van Kuren and his two children there were two other persons in the company; Mr. Reed, the tutor, a tall, grave young man who talked but little, and seemed to watch

Harry with much care, and a delicate, nervous lady, a sister of Mr. Van Kuren's, whom the children called Aunt Emma, and who retired to her apartment as soon as the cloth was removed.

For such a fine dinner it seemed to Bruce that every thing moved very easily and quietly. There were two men in black coats and white ties who went about noiselessly serving the guests and removing the dishes. Mr. Van Kuren, Miss Van Kuren and Mr. Reed drank wine, but there were no glasses at either Harry's or Laura's plate. Mr. Van Kuren asked Bruce if he would like a little claret, and he declined. He began to explain why he did not wish any, but stopped suddenly, feeling perhaps that he was saying too much, but Mr. Van Kuren helped him out with a kindly, smiling inquiry, and he went on: "Chief Trask of my battalion advised me not to drink anything, because he told me that when it was known of a young fireman that he did not take a drop of anything it was a great aid to him and helped him to get along."

"Very good indeed," said Mr. Van Kuren approvingly, "at any rate you're too young now to need it."

At first, the young visitor was not quite sure of himself and did not know exactly what to do with all the forks that he found beside his plate. but by carefully watching his host he managed to acquit himself with credit, and when they arose from the table he realized that he had not made one single "bad break" as Harry would have called it.

"Did you ask Papa about the Dexter house?" whispered Laura at the first opportunity.

"No," replied the boy simply, "I was too much afraid of him; after what you told about his getting mad, I wouldn't have said anything about Mr. Dexter for a hundred dollars."

Soon after dinner Bruce took his leave, having promised his new friends that he would pay them another visit as soon as he could. As he was saying good-bye, Laura slipped into his hand a small piece of paper, and when he opened it in the elevated train he found the following note:

"I have a splendid idea and will let you know about it very soon. I think it will help you to solve the mystery of the haunted house.

"Truly your friend,
LAURA VAN KUREN.

Chapter X.

ONE afternoon Mr. Peter Dewsnap was seated in the great library in which he passed most of his leisure time, busily engaged on a work in which he had taken a great deal of interest. A tap on the door interrupted his labor, and in response to his invitation Bruce Decker entered the room, cap in hand, and saluted him.

"Ah, it's you, young Decker, is it?" said the old gentleman, as he rose to greet his visitor. "Well, how is the chief to-day?"

"He's very well," answered the boy, in hesitating tones, "and the fact is it was at his advice that I accepted your invitation to come up and see your library."

"Very glad to see you, indeed, my young friend," responded the old gentleman, cordially. "As you said yourself the other day I'm an old fire crank, and I like nothing better than talking to young men of your age about what I think is the most important branch of public service in the country. Sit down here, Decker, and if you've an hour to spare it won't do you

Bruce in Mr. Dewsnap's 'fire library.'—
Page 79.

any harm to hear an old man talk about a subject that's nearest to his heart."

Bruce seated himself in one of the big leather arm chairs and glanced about the room. He had never seen as many books in handsome bindings in all his life, and he was particularly struck with the fact that one side of the room was completely filled with oaken shelves containing only books bound in red morocco. About the room were also scattered a number of old colored prints representing, for the most part, pictures of fires and of engines.

"Those books in red constitute my fire library," said Mr. Dewsnap, "and I am proud to say that it is one of the best, if not the very best, in this country. I have books in French, German and English, for you know that the service has a much greater literature than most people have any idea of."

Then Mr. Dewsnap lit a cigar, puffed thoughtfully at it for a moment or two, and went on: "The trouble with most of the boys who want to become firemen is that they are so carried away with the idea of jumping out of bed at a moment's notice and tearing away through the streets at full gallop, and then turning streams on the flames and climbing up ladders and all the rest of it, that they entirely forget the fact that there is a serious side to it all, and that being a good fireman involves more in the way of training, both physical and mental, than almost any other public career that is open to them.

"As I told you the other day, people have been in the habit, or to speak more correctly, were in the habit during the ante-bellum days, of regarding firemen as a lot of toughs and loafers who got together to have a good time and a big hurrah, and sometimes even for political purposes, and comparatively few really knew what a fireman's life meant. Well, when you look at those books there, many of which were written by people of the highest eminence in science or literature, you realize that there must be something in the art of overcoming the most destructive and dangerous of all the elements to excite the attention and enlist the brains of these men. Now take this book for example and glance through it."

Bruce took a large flat volume which Mr. Dewsnap handed him, opened it, and glanced attentively at some of its copper plates. They represented men in quaint, old-fashioned costumes, engaged in putting out fires by the most primitive of means, chiefly by leather buckets passed from hand to hand. The book, as Mr. Dewsnap explained, was printed in 1735 in Holland by Jan vander Heiden, the first inventor of flexible hose. It was an exhaustive treatise on conflagrations and the art of extinguishing them.

"What did they make the hose of in those days?" asked Bruce, as he studied the old-fashioned prints with deep attention.

"Leather," replied Mr. Dewsnap. "And leather continued to be used until forty years ago. In fact, it's used to a great extent to this very day in the smaller towns and cities where fires are of rare occurrence. There are some men who claim that it is better than rubber because it lasts longer and does not rot so easily, but I just showed you that book because its pictures would give you some idea of the enormous advancement that has been made in the last century and a half. Here's another book written in German that is devoted entirely to the burning of the Theatre Comique in Paris a few years ago. Four books in all have been written and published on that subject alone, but strange to say, no book has yet been written in regard to the burning of the Brooklyn Theatre, which was a catastrophe involving an infinitely greater loss of life. It is interesting, by the way, to know that every great fire teaches us some important lesson, and the direct result of the Brooklyn Theatre fire was a number of new laws which govern the construction of theatres, and provides for various improvements and appliances for safety that had never been thought of before."

"Why is it," inquired Bruce, "that so many of these books seem to be by French, German or English authors, instead of by Americans? It seems to me that as we have the best department in the world, the best books on the subject ought to be by American writers."

Mr. Dewsnap smiled broadly at the boy's remark. "That's a very pertinent question, my lad," he said, "and the answer to it is simply this: Those foreigners are more given to writing and talking and thinking than we are. Here we go ahead and do things without stopping to write books about them. I'm expecting some foreigners here within a short time, and when they come I shall take them down to call on Chief Trask. If you see them, you will understand what I mean when I speak of the difference between Americans and either Germans or Englishmen."

"What do you consider the greatest improvement that has been made in the department in your recollection?" asked the boy.

"Well, to my mind, though I would not have admitted it twenty years ago, I think that the fact that politics has been eliminated from the department is one of the chief things that we have to be thankful for, and I believe that it is almost the first time in the history of the world that a fire department has been run without mixing it with political affairs. Why, before the birth of Christ, the Emperor Pompey once refused to allow a new fire company to be formed in Rome because he knew that it was merely an excuse to get together a new crowd of his political opponents, and in the old days when I used to run with a company, politics and the fire department were very much mixed up. I could give you the names of dozens of men who have reached the highest offices in the city and have climbed all the way up by means of their connection with the fire department. Some of these were good men and others were not. But nowadays when a lad like yourself enters the service he sees nothing ahead of him except that service, and the consequence is if he stays in it he devotes himself to his duties with no object in view except to become chief of the department. At least that's what he ought to do.

"But for all its politics and its toughs, the members of the old department had just as much pluck and were just as ready to take the hose nozzle in hand and go right into a burning building as they are to-day. I've shown you these books, my boy, because I wanted you to feel that there was a dignity in the service to which you intend to devote yourself, and if you want to rise in it, it must be by hard work, obedience to orders, and constant study. Don't be afraid to borrow some of these books of me to read when you have nothing else to do. There are plenty of them that are in English that you could learn something from. It's education nowadays that tells. But I've a project in my mind that both Mr. Trask and I have devoted considerable time to, and I hope to live to see the day when it will be carried out. I want to see a school established in which boys like yourself can be trained for the fire department just as they are trained for the navy. My idea would be to take a number of boys every year from the public schools in the city and give them a regular course of training in gymnastics and special scientific studies so that by the time they were twenty-one they would be much better prepared to fight fire than are the young men that usually join the department at that age."

"That's a magnificent idea;" cried Bruce with an enthusiasm that was so hearty and genuine that the old gentleman was delighted, "and I can tell you one thing, and that is you wouldn't have any difficulty in getting scholars for it. It seems to me that every boy in New York is just as crazy to run to fires as I was when I lived in the country. Why, do you know sir, that every time we start out of quarters there's such a swarm of young ones in the street that it's a wonder we don't run over two or three of them. And besides, boys seem to me to be tougher and more supple than men. There are lots of things I can do in an athletic way that Tom Brophy can't and he's twenty-five years old."

"Well," said the old gentleman pleasantly, "you ask some of the lads of your acquaintance how they'd like to join such a school as that and put down on paper any ideas you may have regarding it. Then the next time I see you we will talk them over."

As Bruce walked slowly homeward after one of the pleasantest hours he had spent since his arrival in the city, he felt a new pride which he had never known before, in the great department which it was his wish to serve. The fact that fire departments had existed since the earliest times had never occurred to him, and he determined to devote all his leisure time to a study of Mr. Dewsnap's pet scheme of a training school in the hope that he might be able to render the kindly old gentlemen some service which he would appreciate.

Chapter XI.

IT was not at all unnatural that Bruce Decker should cherish in his heart a strong desire to go to a fire as one of the members of the truck company. This longing grew stronger in his heart every day, and when the opportunity did come it found him, fortunately enough, ready to make the most of it.

It happened one warm day in August, that three or four of the men were absent on their summer's vacation and one or two others because of illness, and while the company was thus crippled, Charley Weyman fell and hurt his right arm so badly that the chief advised him to go around to the nearest doctor's and have it dressed. As the injured fireman left the quarters, his superior turned to Bruce and said, " My boy, you see how short-handed we are to-day ; now do you think that if an alarm should come in you could take Weyman's place on the driver's seat ? "

The boy's eyes brightened and there was an eager look in his face as he made answer, " I'm sure I could and I only wish that an alarm would come in."

"All right," said the chief "just keep yourself in readiness for we can never know when there is an alarm coming."

Then he went up stairs, and Bruce stepped out into the street, and looked up and down it as far as his eye could reach as if he expected to see the smoke and flame bursting out from some building within his range of vision. But the sun poured down on his bare head, and he was soon glad to retreat to the shade of the quarters, where he stood idly looking at the brass gongs, and wondering how soon they would begin to ring out their tale of smoke, flame and disaster.

And then the thought occurred to him that he had no right to stand there wishing for a fire which might bring ruin and death to his fellow creatures, and could benefit no one but himself; and it was not at all certain that it would benefit even him. So he satisfied his conscience by changing the form although not the tenor of his thoughts. "I wish," he said to himself "that if it were necessary for the world's good to have a fire to-day that it might be right here within this district. There's no harm in wishing that I'm sure. Of course I wouldn't like to have any people killed at the fire or to have any poor man lose all his furniture and clothes, but there are fires every day, and this is the first time I've ever had a chance—"

"Clang! clang!" rang out the brass gong at his side, and never, since the first time that he heard an alarm ring, had the sound of the bell stirred him with such excitement as it did now.

His opportunity had come at last, and without a moment's delay he clambered up over the wheel of the truck and dropped into the driver's seat.

He knew that some of the men were racing in from the back room, that others were sliding down the brass poles, and that two of them were already at the horses' heads, while another was adjusting the harness on the chief's wagon.

And all this time Bruce was saying to himself, "Now, I'm going to keep cool, no matter what happens, and I'll not spoil the greatest chance of my life by getting nervous."

It was with this thought in his mind that he seized the reins and waited quietly until the men had snapped the collars about the horses' necks and fastened the reins to their bits. Meantime the brass gong had been ringing the number of the station, and the boy, with his wits entirely about him, was keeping count of the strokes.

"One, two, three — one, two — one, two, three, four, that's 324," he said to himself as he tightened the reins, while the men gave the eager horses their heads and sprang up on the truck.

Bruce knew where station No. 324 was, for he had long since familiarized himself thoroughly with the district in which the company was located, so as he passed over the threshold he gave the horses their heads, and turning sharply to the right was soon on his way to the densely populated east side region in which the fire was raging.

Chief Trask, seated in his little wagon, passed him before he had reached the first corner, his horse going at full gallop, and the gong in the dashboard ringing out its sharp warnings. As the chief went by he turned his head and saw his young protege sitting bolt upright in Weyman's seat, looking carefully ahead of him, and keeping his horses well in hand although they were going at almost their best speed. The boy seemed perfectly cool, and it was apparent to the superior officer that he knew what his duty was and proposed to perform it. Then the chief took the lead, and as they passed the first street, the engine and tender, with Captain Murphy in command,

Down this thoroughfare for three blocks—and never in his life had Bruce known such a reckless ride.—*Page 91*.

came thundering along, turned the corner, and fell in behind them. Now they turned into a crowded thoroughfare where the people, warned by the sharp clanging of the gong in the chief's wagon, hastily made way for the flying battalion. Down this thoroughfare for three blocks—and never in his life had Bruce known such a reckless ride—then another sharp turn carried them into full view of the fire.

The upper story of a factory was ablaze, and in the street in front of it two policemen were vainly trying to keep back an excited throng of people, many of whom were yelling and gesticulating and talking in German and Polish, while others were weeping from sheer excitement. The chief was on the sidewalk in a moment and, in an incredibly short space of time, the crowd had been driven away to a respectful distance, the hose attached to a hydrant across the street and run rapidly out to a convenient length, while the members of the truck company, acting under their chief's order, were quickly and quietly getting their ladders against the front of the building and preparing to ascend. Bruce did not know exactly what he was expected to do, but concluded that it would be best for him to sit where he was and take care of his horses. From his place in the driver's seat he noted carefully the speedy, intelligent and systematic work of the brigade. He saw the chief of battalion cast his practiced eye at the building and then tell his men where to direct the streams of water. In less than two minutes the flames were under control, and the frightened people, who had been screaming and crying in the street, realized that what they had mistaken for an awful conflagration was in reality nothing but a comparatively harmless combustion in the factory's upper floor, that no lives had been jeopardized, and that all danger of the flames spreading had vanished in the face of the rapid and efficient work of Chief Trask's men.

The neighborhood was inhabited chiefly by foreigners, and Bruce could hear these people talking to one another in half a dozen strange tongues, as they leaned out of windows or crowded about the engines as closely as the police would allow them. And among this crowd of chattering, excited aliens, Bruce noticed one man of striking appearance, who seemed totally different from those about him, and who stood on the steps of a tenement house and watched the fire with amusement and interest reflected on his countenance.

In marked contrast to the other denizens of the street, this man was well dressed and carried with him an unmistakable air of prosperity. He was tall and dark, and his heavy black beard was cropped close to his face. As he stood on the top step the boy could see his profile, distinctly. It was clear cut, the nose slightly aquiline and the chin and mouth firm and square. He wondered idly what this well-dressed man could be doing in that part of the city, and, while he was still wondering, the subject of his thoughts came down the steps and walked quickly away, for by this time the fire was out, the men were reeling up the hose, and the members of the truck company were returning their apparatus to the truck and preparing to go home.

At the same time the uniformed employees of the insurance patrol placed themselves in the doorways of the factory and Chief Trask came over to where Bruce was sitting with his horses and bade him start for home. As they drove slowly in the direction of the quarters they passed the tall man with the close cropped black beard. He eyed them sharply, as they went by, and as he turned his face, Bruce noticed what he had not observed before, namely, a long scar which ran obliquely across his chin.

Just at this moment he heard one of the men on the truck behind him say to his fellow: "There's that tall, ugly looking chap that used to come round to the quarters every once and a while, I haven't seen him for six months now, and I don't know that I want to see him again, for I never liked his looks." Bruce eagerly turned his head for a final glimpse of the dark stranger, but he had disappeared.

"Never mind," he said to himself, "that face is fixed in my mind and I'll never forget it. One of these days I'll find out who that man is, and what he had to do with my father."

That afternoon he sat in his accustomed corner in the back room of the quarters, thinking over his day's experience. He was very quiet and did not join in the conversation that was going on around him. He wanted to tell his friend, Weyman, about the tall stranger with the scar on his chin, and he would have done so, had it not been that he remembered Laura's emphatic order not to allow any one but herself to share his secret.

For fully half an hour he thought the matter over, and then determined, reluctantly it must be owned, not to say anything about it to Weyman, until he had obtained the young girl's permission.

And it was just at this stage of his investigations that he made his first serious blunder. If he had gone at once to his friend and told him about the man whom he had seen down among the Poles and Russians and Germans, in the tenement house quarter of the town, it would have made a great difference in his life. But he allowed himself to be influenced by a pretty, imperious, spoiled little girl, instead of by a quick-witted, sensible and devoted friend, with results which will be described in future chapters of this story.

Chapter XII.

CHARLEY WEYMAN was anxious to learn how his boy friend had been received and entertained in the Van Kuren mansion, and he listened attentively while Bruce described his visit, told him how friendly Laura and Harry had been, and with what courtesy he had been welcomed by their father and their aunt, but somehow he neglected to mention his long conversation with Laura in the summer-house, nor did he refer to the Dexter mansion at all. The young girl's words still rang in his ears, and it was a pleasant thought to him that he had a secret to share with her, a secret which none of his other friends need know about. The little scrawl which she had placed in his hand at parting he kept in the innermost compartment of his pocket book, and many a time during the day while engaged at his work he would take the little crumpled bit of paper out or its hiding place, read it carefully through and then return it, carefully folded up.

And as he did so, he would wonder for the thousandth time what her splendid idea could be, and how it could help him to solve the mystery of what she called the "haunted house." It was just a week after his visit to the Van Kuren's that he entered the quarters and found a letter addressed to him lying on the table in the back room. He recognized the handwriting at once, and was conscious of a faint color that crept into his cheeks as he seized the precious missive and went upstairs to read it. This is what he found when he tore off the envelope. It was carefully written in pencil on a sheet of paper, which looked as if it had been torn out of a school copy book.

"Bruce Decker, Esq.

Dear Friend: I have found out where my old nurse lives, and perhaps if you go to see her she will tell you what you want to know. Don't tell her that you know me, or that you were ever at our house, but ask her about Mr. Dexter and why he lives there all by himself. I think there is an awful mystery about it all, and perhaps some day you will be the hero of a story that will tell about it.

"When are you coming up to see us again? Good-bye now, for the present. Your true friend,

Laura VanKuren.

P. S.—I heard papa say that you seemed to be a very nice boy.

P. S.—I forgot to tell you about Ann's address. She lives at ooo Ave. A, and her name is Mrs. Ann Crehan."

Bruce was not long in making his way to the address given in Laura's letter. Mrs. Crehan seemed to be nearly a hundred years old, and was certainly very deaf. He succeeded after a while in making her understand what he wanted.

"Aye, aye, sir," she said, "Shure they were good people, too, for all the master had his quarrel with them, but there's none left now except the ould gentleman, for his son went away and never came back."

"But what was the quarrel about?" bawled the boy at the top of his lungs.

"What was the quarrel about?" repeated the old woman. "Why it was about family matters, of course. What else do people quarrel about?"

"But can't you remember what sort of family matters they were?" persisted Bruce.

"No, sir, I cannot," rejoined the old woman, with a look of fox-like cunning on her face; "and if I could I'd not be talking about it either. What right have I, who was a servant in the family of Mr. VanKuren, and of his wife that's dead and gone—may the Lord have mercy on her soul—this ten year come next January, what right have I to be gossiping with the likes of you about their private matters? No, young

She seemed to be nearly a hundred years old, and she was certainly very deaf.—*Page 98.*

man, ye'll get nothing out of Ann Crehan about the VanKurens, or the Dexters, or any other of the rale quality that we had in thim days when I went out to service."

For half an hour Bruce vainly endeavored to elicit from the old woman some facts regarding the history of the Dexter family. Sometimes she seemed on the point of telling something, and then the old look of cunning would come back to her wrinkled face, and she would shake her head and chuckle, declaring that she knew her place and nothing could induce her to gossip about her old master or his family affairs.

He even went so far as to ask her if she remembered a tall, dark bearded man with a scar across his chin, who used to visit the family, occasionally, but at this inquiry the old woman became very angry and declared that he was an impertinent young spalpeen to come into a decent body's house and attempt to pry into matters that did not concern him. She said, moreover, that she was going to tell Mr. Dexter himself, the next time he came to see her— "and he might be here any minute," she added—and the boy on hearing this threat, departed with much speed, and slunk cautiously along the street, looking on every side for Mr. Samuel Dexter.

Charley Weyman told Bruce that he had read in a "Complete Handbook of Etiquette" that it was ordained by the leaders of fashion that any one entertained at a dinner party should make what is known as a "dinner call" within a week or ten days after the dinner. Therefore he advised the young boy to present himself at the Van Kuren mansion some afternoon, in acknowledgment of the courtesy which had been shown him.

Bruce, who had been trying for three days to contrive some plausible pretext for going up to that part of the town again, was only too glad to hear this, and that very afternoon, having first secured Mr. Trask's permission, he made himself as neat as he possibly could, and started on the elevated train.

Never before had a journey by steam seemed to him as long as this one. He counted the blocks as they passed beneath him, and rejoiced to think that every minute lessened the distance between him and the young girl who was now occupying a large share of his thoughts. As he approached the Van Kuren mansion, he strained his eyes to look over the hedge that separated the lawn from the highway, hoping that he might catch a glimpse of Laura somewhere in the grounds.

He was not disappointed. Just as he passed through the gate, he caught sight of some one seated in the summer-house—the very one in which he had had his long talk on the occasion of his first visit—and then it seemed to him that this some one looked up for a moment, recognized him, and then became absorbed in the pages of a book. It was Laura; but although his feet sounded noisily on the gravel-walk she did not look up, and when at last he stopped, a little embarrassed, at the step of the summer-house, lifted his hat, and addressed her by name, she started as suddenly as if she had been awakened from a dream, and then, so it seemed to him, recognized him with much surprise.

She asked him to sit down, which he did, placing himself at the very edge of a rustic bench and holding his hat awkwardly over his knees. Then she laid her book down on the table in the middle of the house, with the leaves open at the place where she had been reading, a proceeding which somehow gave to her visitor the impression that she hoped to resume it again at an early moment. This, taken in connection with a certain cool reserve in her manner, which was altogether different from what he had experienced at her hands before, acted like a cold chill upon the young man—which was precisely the effect which she had reckoned on.

The truth is that Laura, like a great many of the most charming of her sex, was a natural born coquette, and, having noticed how eagerly her young admirer responded to her advances on the occasion of their first meeting, she took pleasure in treating him now with a degree of indifference which led him to fear that he had in some way managed to offend her.

Bruce had had very little experience with girls, and for that reason he felt chilled and hurt at the manifest change in Laura's voice and manner. If he had known a little more of the sex he would have been very much flattered to think that this clever, brilliant and fascinating young beauty—for such Laura really was—should have taken the trouble to play upon his feelings at all. And if, moreover, Bruce had dreamt of the amount of interest that he had awakened in her, he would have been that afternoon the most jubilant young man in the whole city. She had been thinking of hardly anything but the romantic history of the good-looking, modest, young fire laddie, and she was at this very moment fairly burning to know if he had found out anything more about the mystery which enveloped his origin and in which it seemed to her that somehow her own friends were associated. If she could only find out why her father had quarreled with Mr. Dexter, she might be able to help him and perhaps to make him comprehend why the old doorway had looked so familiar.

For a few minutes the two conversed, stiffly, about matters in which neither had any real interest, for all the world as if they had been full grown people, instead of a mere boy and girl. Then Laura saw that her guest was too shy to broach the topic which was uppermost in the minds of both, and so she relented a little, smiled quite pleasantly, but not too pleasantly, and asked him with assumed carelessness if he had found out anything more about his mysterious origin.

"No," replied Bruce, but with a note of hesitation in his voice, which served to whet Laura's curiosity to such a degree that she exclaimed, bluntly, "Do tell me if you went to see old Ann, and what she said to you; I am just dying to know."

Her enthusiasm cheered Bruce enormously and restored a good deal of the self-confidence which had disappeared when he believed that he had somehow offended her.

"I went to see her," he said, "but I really could not get anything out of her, for she's very old and deaf, and seems to be actuated by but one motive, which is to keep to herself whatever matters of family history she may have learned while she was in your father's employ. I think she knows something about that Mr. Dexter and the reason of the family quarrel, and she might possibly talk to you about it, but she looked upon me as an impertinent stranger, and I could get nothing out of her. But there was something that happened the other day that might or might not lead to some further developments. But I suppose if I were to tell you, you would repeat it to your father or to Harry——"

"Go on this minute, and tell me! You know perfectly well we're not either one of us to talk to anybody about our secret. Just let me once catch you telling, that's all. Now go on."

"Well," continued Bruce, highly elated by the young girl's interest in him and her return to her old manner, "the other day there was a fire down in a part of the city where it's nothing but tenement houses and factories and where nobody but foreigners live. I drove the hook and ladder truck, of course," the boy inflated his chest, proudly, as he said this, "and while I was sitting there looking at the fire I saw a well-dressed gentleman with a black beard, standing on the step of one of the tenement houses. As we were driving home slowly we passed him again, and a couple of the men on the truck saw him, too. Who do you think he was?"

"I don't know, tell me quick!" cried Laura who was listening with breathless interest and cheeks flushed with more than their natural color.

"I noticed," continued Bruce in dramatic tones, "that he had a long scar across his chin——"

"Mercy!" gasped Laura. "It must have been that fearful man you told me about who used to come down to see your father. If we could only find him, the mystery would be solved."

"But I couldn't get off the truck, and so I had to go back to the quarters without learning anything more," said Bruce sadly, and just then Harry came whooping across the lawn, seized Bruce by both hands, waltzed him out of the summer-house and succeeded in throwing him on his back on the grass before the astonished boy fairly realized what had happened. This was Harry's exuberant way of welcoming a friend, and a moment later he had Bruce on his feet again and was helping to rub the dust and the grass stains from his clothes.

Of course Harry's advent put an immediate stop to the conversation and half an hour later Harry proposed that they should all go out for a walk.

"You'd better not unless you've got your lesson, Mr. Harry, I can tell you that," said his sister in warning accents, "you know what will happen the next time you're caught running off without doing your work first."

"Oh, bother the lessons" cried the boy carelessly, I can do them after I get back."

Ten minutes later as they were walking quietly along the highway Bruce suddenly fell behind the others a step, seized Laura's arm in one hand and with the other pointed to a man who had just passed them, driving a fine pair of black horses.

Laura looked at the driver and then at Bruce in a surprised way and then seemed to signal with her lips "who is he?"

In reply Bruce simply drew his finger slowly down his chin and Laura, catching his meaning at once, leaped excitedly on to a stone wall beside the road and gazed after the retreating buggy, straining her eyes to get a full, fair view of its occupant.

"What's the matter with you Laura?" demanded her brother brusquely, "you're getting too old to be hopping up on stone walls, I can tell you."

Laura descended to the path again and walked quietly along with the two boys, not deigning to make any response to Harry's criticism.

Chapter XIII.

FOR a few moments after Laura had descended from the wall the trio walked along in silence. Bruce, who had been really startled by the sudden apparition of the black-bearded man, was too busy with his own thoughts to do much talking. What did the presence of this mysterious stranger in that part of the town signify? Could it be that he was following up the boy just as he had followed up the father? Bruce could not drive from his mind the remembrance of what Weyman had told him, and now, whenever he thought of his father, he remembered that on the very day when he went to his death in the smoke and the flames of the Broadway fire that same bearded stranger had called to see him and they had had a long, earnest talk together.

And now, twice within a week, the stranger's path had crossed that of the boy. Was this a mere accident or was he deliberately shadowing the young lad with a view to wreaking further vengeance on him? As for Laura, she was fairly bubbling over with excitement, but she said nothing for fear of awakening her brother's suspicion. She wished that she could devise some excuse for getting him out of the way, if only for a few minutes, in order that she might have a few words with Bruce, and so as they paused for a moment at a turn in the road, she said innocently: "You see that fence down there by the brook? Well, Tommy Martin ran and jumped over it the other day and leaped clean on the other side of the brook. He's the best jumper anywhere around here."

Now, Tommy Martin was a boy who lived near them and who often came over to visit them—a boy of whom Harry was decidedly jealous, partly because they had already been looked upon as rivals in such sports as running and jumping, and partly because they both liked the same girl, Kitty Harriott, a particular friend of Laura's. Laura knew all about this rivalry when she took pains to point out the fence and brook over which Tommy had leaped so brilliantly, and she was not surprised when Harry burst forth contemptuously: "What do you mean by the best jumper anywhere about here? You don't call that anything of a jump, do you? Why that's nothing at all. I can go over it myself and I'll bet I'll strike two feet further on the other side than Tom did!"

With these words he slipped off his coat, walked over toward the spot indicated by his sister, surveyed it carefully and then walked back a dozen paces in order to make a flying leap. While he was doing this Laura had gasped out to Bruce, "Was that really the man with the black beard and the scar that went by?"

"Yes," replied the boy, "I'd know him anywhere I saw him. Did you get a fair look at him?"

"Not very," answered Laura, "but I think I would know him again if I saw him. Wasn't that neat, the way I got Harry away for a minute? Now, you must be sure not to say a word to him or to anybody else about that man. We'll keep that a secret for ourselves. My! just look at Harry, he's going to take that jump. The silly fool, Tommy never jumped over that, I just told Harry that so as to get him out of the way a minute. He thinks he can do everything that Tommy does and they're both of them perfectly wild over the same girl, who is my dearest friend. I've told her all about you, and she's just crazy to see you."

At this moment Harry leaped boldly over the fence and landed on the other side, but not quite where he had expected. Either the brook was wider than he supposed or else his foot slipped, but somehow, instead of alighting on the grassy bank he struck in about two feet of water, clutched wildly at the branch of an overhanging tree and then fell over on his back. Laura began to laugh, but Bruce, fearing that his friend might have been hurt by his fall, ran down to help him. He crossed the fence just as Harry climbed up on the shore sputtering and blowing and wiping the mud and water from his face. He was completely soaked, and his cap was drifting rapidly down stream.

"Are you hurt?" demanded Bruce anxiously.

"No, of course I'm not, but I'll bet you Tommy Martin never made that jump; Laura just said that to get me into the water. Never mind she'll catch it when we get home. What are you laughing at up there?" he continued, turning suddenly and addressing himself to his sister who was standing by the roadside with amusement pictured on her face. "Perhaps you won't think it so funny after a while," continued the boy, angrily, and then Bruce, fearing that he too might be moved to laughter by his comical appearance, ran off down the stream to recover the lost cap.

Harry was soaking wet, and there was nothing for him to do but take off his coat and waistcoat and place them on a big rock on which the sun had been shining all day, while he himself sat down beside them, wrung the water out of his trousers and began to dry off. He was in the midst of the drying process when Bruce said to Laura in a low whisper, "I've just got an idea in my head about that man. Doesn't Mr. Dexter live near here?"

"Yes," replied the young girl, "about a quarter of a mile further on."

"Then he was going that way when he passed us, wasn't he?"

"Certainly he was; why I wonder if it could be possible that he was going up there. Do let us hurry on."

"I do believe that you two have got some sort of a secret between you," exclaimed Harry, suddenly looking up. "What man are you talking about? I tell you you'd better let me know all about it."

"Secret," said Laura, slyly, "there's no secret in what I was saying, because everybody knows it. I was just telling him about Kitty and you, and there's lots more things I could tell him if I wanted to."

Harry dropped the conversation at this point, and a minute or two later he picked up his coat and vest, declared that he was dry enough anyway and proposed that they should continue their walk. In a few minutes he had completely recovered his good humor and offered Bruce to run him a race to the next gateway. Bruce accepted the challenge, never doubting that he could win it, but he found to his surprise that the slim, active, young New Yorker was a much fleeter runner than he was, and, do what he could, strain every nerve as he might, he reached the goal completely out of breath and fully fifty feet behind his adversary, whom he found standing by the gate post looking, as he expressed it, "as fresh as a daisy," and laughing all over at his own success.

Bruce was just a little bit annoyed to find himself so easily beaten by a lad whose appearance indicated anything but strength and agility, but when he saw how the little bit of excitement and the triumph of winning the race had restored his friend's temper to its usual good-natured pitch and completely dispelled a feeling which might have culminated in a quarrel, he was rather glad on the whole that he himself had lost.

Therefore he simply smiled pleasantly, and said what was perfectly true : "Well, I never thought you could run like that."

Then they sat down on the big, white marble carriage block and waited for Laura, whom they could see approaching at a leisurely pace. Bruce realized, as he looked about him, that they were not far from the Dexter mansion. In fact, by going out in the middle of the road, he could easily see the dark clump of firs and pines and the grey gate posts which guarded the entrance. As they walked along he and Laura exchanged significant glances from time to time and as they drew near to the house, he said to Harry, "That's the house I went to for those magazines and papers that day I met you."

"Why, do you know old man Dexter?" demanded the boy with much interest.

"No," said Bruce, "except that he was very nice to me that day. Did you ever meet him?"

"Not for a long while," replied Harry.

"Let's all go into the grounds and see what the place looks like," said Laura.

"You'd better not, Laura, said her brother, significantly, "we'll be sure to be caught if we do, and you know perfectly well what papa said would happen if he heard of our going there."

"Well, I've a great mind to go in there and ask Mr. Dexter if he has any more magazines for us," said Bruce, bravely. "I'm not afraid of those thick woods, and I'm not afraid of him either. Come along, let's all go in there."

"I'd just as leave go," said Laura, defiantly, "even if we were told not to, but listen, there comes somebody now." They had just reached the gateway by this time and as they peered through it into the shadowy depths of the fir woods, they heard the quick hoof-beats of approaching horses, and in another moment a buggy drawn by two black horses, came down through the grounds at a swift pace and passed through the gateway into the road. The tall, bearded and scarred stranger held the reins and beside him sat Mr. Samuel Dexter. Laura held her breath with excitement, and an eager gleam came into Bruce's eyes as he turned significantly toward her. Another link had been added to the chain in which he was trying to connect the past with the present. Mr. Dexter and the mysterious one were evidently friends, and he resolved that the very next day he would go to him, tell him his own history as far as he knew of it, and ask him to help him solve the remainder of it.

"What are you going to do?" whispered Laura, excitedly. Bruce made no reply except to shake his head and place his fingers on his lips as if to command silence.

Chapter XIV.

"I'D like to know what's come over that boy lately," said Tom Brophy, one morning. as he pointed to Bruce, who was standing idly by the wall with his broom in his hand gazing vacantly into space instead of attending to his work.

"I don't know rejoined Weyman, "but my opinion is that he's in love. When he first came here, he was as active and steady a lad as one would expect to see, but within a fortnight or so he has changed tremendously. You see he got acquainted with a young chap up town, and he's been up there two or three times to visit him. This other boy's father is well fixed, and the first time Bruce went up there he came back crazy over the big house and the servants and horses and all the rest of it. He'll make a big mistake if he tries to fly too high."

"Well, all I've got to say is this," observed Brophy, "that if he don't mind his eye he'll have the chief jumping on him some day with both feet, and when the chief jumps on a man he's liable to know it.

Both Weyman and Brophy were right in regard to the young boy. He had altered materially since his acquaintance with Harry and Laura Van Kuren. It had made him dissatisfied to see children of his own age living in the style that he had never dreamt of before, and he could not help asking himself why it was that he, Bruce Decker, should be obliged to look after horses, and run errands for the chief of a fire battalion while Harry, who was neither better nor cleverer than he was, had a pony of his own to ride, wore good clothes every day, and in short, lived upon the very fat of the land; and this problem, which he put to himself very often now, always led him to speculate as to his own origin, and to wonder whether Laura could be right in her belief that he was being unjustly kept out of innumerable good things that rightfully belonged to him.

Charley Weyman, who was a close observer and took a deep interest in the son of his old friend, was right in his surmise that Bruce was in love, although the boy himself would have been very much surprised if he had been told of it. Never in all his life had he met any girl as pretty, as well-bred and as charming as Laura Van Kuren. She seemed to him to have no fault, except perhaps her habit of quarreling with her brother, but that was an occurrence of such frequency that Bruce had become accustomed to it and was no longer surprised when the two children fell out. He had noticed, too, that they never "stayed mad" with one another, to use an expressive phrase in vogue among children, and although he had once seen Laura so far forget the ethics of society as to hurl a half a brick at her brother's head, he noticed that within five minutes afterward they were playing together as happily as if nothing had happened. And then what boy could resist a girl who took as deep an interest in him as Laura did in the young fireman?

Why, she even took a much deeper interest in solving what she called, quoting from one of her favorite romances "the mystery that shrouded his birth" than he did himself, and if it had not been for her active co-operation and sympathy he was sure that the incident of the old doorway of the Dexter mansion would have passed from his mind without his making any effort to learn its significance.

Moreover, the novelty of life in the great city was beginning to wear off, and he could not deny that his work at quarters was becoming a trifle irksome to him. It was always the same thing, rubbing down the horses, cleaning out their stalls, waiting in the building while the men were away and now and then doing an errand for Chief Trask or Charley Weyman. He had not even been allowed to go to a fire since the important day when he drove the truck down to the tenement house region and beheld for the first time the tall man with the black beard and the scarred face.

He was thinking of all these things and some others besides as he stood leaning against the wall with his broom in his hand, and as he resumed his work with a discontented sigh, he determined to take the first opportunity to go up town and ask Mr. Dexter about the man with whom he had seen him driving. He had to wait nearly a week before he could get an afternoon off, and a very long week it seemed to him, too. Finally, one bright afternoon saw him speeding northward on the elevated railroad, his face bright at the prospect of seeing Laura and his heart beating with excitement as he thought of the interview which he had planned.

He had determined to go at first to the Van Kuren's, because Laura had charged him so solemnly not to do anything in the matter without first consulting her, that he felt that it would be absolute treachery on his part to ask the all-important question unless he had first obtained her permission.

Descending the steps of the elevated station, he started at a brisk walk in the direction of his friend's house, and what was his surprise and delight on turning the first corner to find himself face to face with both children who, accompanied by Mr. Reed, the tutor, were just starting for a long walk. They hailed him with boisterous delight and Bruce, having first bowed with much deference to Mr. Reed, of whom he stood in considerable awe, shook hands with both Laura and Harry and told them that he was just on his way to call on them.

"We are just going out for a walk Master Decker," said Mr. Reed, "and we would be very glad to have you accompany us." Mr. Reed would not have invited any of the boys in the neighborhood to go with them, but he had been struck with the respectful manner in which Bruce had lifted his cap to him. Then they all set off together, Bruce and Harry marching ahead, while the tutor brought up in the rear with Laura.

"Which way shall we go to-day?" said Harry, turning to the tutor, and at the same moment Bruce contrived to throw a significant glance at Laura, a glance which the young girl comprehended at once and which prompted her to exclaim "Oh, let's follow this road along to where we were the other day, Harry, there's a place there with lots of lovely flowers and there's one tree that I don't know the name of and I want to ask Mr. Reed what it is."

"Very well," rejoined the tutor pleasantly, "we'll go where you say, Miss Laura," and Bruce chuckled to himself, as he noticed how the quick-witted girl's tact served his purpose.

They had not gone far before he contrived to fall behind the others with her for a moment, and whisper: "That's just what I wanted; I came up here to go and see that Mr. Dexter, but I wouldn't go until I had told you about it first; I'm going to ask him who that man is he was driving with the other day."

Laura gave him a quick look which expressed her gratitude, and then said: "Be careful not to let Mr. Reed know that we ever talked about this Mr. Dexter before, because it would be awful if papa were to find out that we went as far through the gateway as we did that afternoon. When we get there, just tell him that you have an errand with an old gentleman who lives in the house, and we'll walk along slowly while you're inside. That's the best way."

That ended their conversation and a moment later Bruce and Harry had leaped the fence into an adjoining field, and were down on their knees in the grass hunting for mushrooms. Neither the tutor nor either of the children could distinguish the edible mushrooms from toadstools and other fungi, but Bruce, who had often gathered them near his country home, readily pointed out the difference in appearance and smell between the two. Mr. Reed seemed very much pleased with what the boy told him; for although he was thoroughly well versed in books and a most accomplished classical scholar and instructor, there were a great many things concerning everyday life of which he was ignorant, and it was plain to both of his young pupils that Bruce was rising rapidly in the tutor's esteem. It was not long before they had gathered what the young country boy called "a good mess" of edible fungi, and when he had solemnly certified to the fact that there was not a toadstool in the whole lot, they were wrapped up in a bit of old newspaper and carefully hidden away in a cool, damp spot beside the very brook into which Harry had fallen the week before.

"We'll stop and get them on our return," said the tutor, "and I shall tell Mr. Van Kuren

Bruce delivers a lecture on botany.—*Page 122*.

when they are served at dinner to-night that it was you who showed us how to distinguish them."

They were drawing nearer the Dexter mansion as he said this, and Bruce took occasion to say to the tutor "By the way, I have a little errand here and if you've no objection I would like to stop a few minutes. There is an old gentlemen who sometimes sends magazines and books down to our quarters for the men to read, and I must see him for a moment."

"Certainly," replied the tutor "where does he live?"

"In the next house—that one with the big hedge in front of it," replied the boy.

Mr. Reed stopped short, and the smile disappeared from his face and was replaced by a queer look of annoyance and anxiety.

"Do you mean Mr. Dexter," he asked.

"Yes, sir."

Mr. Reed looked at his watch, and then said quietly: "It's rather later than I thought it was, so I think we will return to the house. We shall walk slowly, so you may overtake us if your visit is not too long, Master Decker."

Bruce and Laura exchanged glances but did not dispute Mr. Reed's order, and then, while the others turned their faces toward their home,

Bruce darted through the gateway, and sped along the winding path through the fir trees.

Ten minutes later, Laura, who had exhausted her ingenuity in devising excuses for delaying their return, heard with delight Bruce's familiar voice behind them, and stopped to wait for him. As he approached she saw that his face, which had been so bright and smiling all the afternoon, was sober and pale now, and the thought flashed across her mind that perhaps he had encountered the ghost of one of his relatives in the old house, some long-veiled woman flitting up and down the old staircase as spirits always did in the romances with which she was familiar.

"Well?" she said, as Bruce joined her

"I was just too late," said the boy with something like a sob in his voice, " Mr. Dexter sailed for Europe yesterday, and there's nobody there but an old couple who are taking care of the house. They don't know when he will be back or anything about it. There goes my last and only chance."

Chapter XV.

ONE afternoon Bruce Decker was seated in front of the quarters reading a newspaper, and waiting for the men to return from a fire to which they had been summoned half an hour before. So engrossed was he that he did not hear the footsteps of three gentlemen who were crossing the street directly in front of him, and he was startled to hear his name suddenly pronounced in a quick, imperious way.

Leaping to his feet he found himself face to face with his kind old friend, Mr. Dewsnap, known to all the members of the company as the "fire crank." Mr. Dewsnap's companions were two gentlemen, both of them well dressed and of prepossessing appearance, and both unquestionably foreigners. One was a tall man, attired in a suit of very large checks, and the other was short, rotund and long haired. The former was evidently an Englishman, and the latter a German.

"Where's the chief?" inquired Mr. Dewsnap.

"Out with the company," replied the boy, taking off his cap, for Bruce had sense enough to know that politeness to his elders was always a strong point in favor of any boy.

"That's too bad," replied Mr. Dewsnap, taking out his watch, "because I have brought down these two gentlemen to show them the way we have in this country of putting out fires, and I wanted to have them make Chief Trask's acquaintance. However," he continued, "I'll just take them inside here and explain what I can myself; then when the chief comes back he can show them the rest."

With these words the three visitors entered the building, and in a moment Mr. Dewsnap was in the midst of a voluble description of the workings of the service. Bruce noticed that both strangers seemed to display a more than ordinary degree of interest, and they both of them took notes of what they heard. Mr. Dewsnap, who knew as much of the department as a good many firemen, talked to them energetically and kept them interested until the company returned from the fire, and Chief Trask, alighting from his wagon, came forward to welcome his visitors. The two visitors were introduced respectively as Baron Bernstoff and the Honorable Rupert Doubter.

"These gentlemen," said Mr. Dewsnap, "have come to this country for the purpose of studying its peculiar institutions, and they are particularly desirous of learning all they can about the Fire Department of New York, the fame of which has spread through every city in Europe. The fact is, that although they are too polite to say so, I am afraid that they do not believe what has been told them in regard to the rapidity with which our companies get out to a fire when the alarm sounds. I've shown them as much as I can about the building and explained to them the way the alarms are sent out, but I just wish you would tell them what you know, and give them a little illustration of how things are done."

Chief Trask, like all efficient members of the service, took a just pride in his work and was never so happy as when expatiating to benighted foreigners on the wonderful efficiency of the fire brigade of New York, as compared with those of the other leading capitals of the world.

"Our motto, gentlemen," said the chief, "is to be always ready for an emergency, and when that emergency comes to meet it without an instant's loss of time. We have just come from a fire about six or eight blocks from here, and now you will see that the men are getting ready for the next alarm."

As he spoke he directed his visitors' attention to the truck, which by this time had been backed carefully into the quarters to its resting place in the centre of the building, while the men were leading the horses slowly up and down the street, to the admiration of a group of small boys who had been attracted to the scene by the return of the apparatus, and were now gazing upon the firemen with that profound respect which a New York boy always entertains for those superior and uniformed beings. The horses were thoroughly rubbed down and then returned to their stalls, and at the same time the men, aided by Bruce, carefully inspected the hook and ladder truck to see that nothing had been broken in their swift run, and then washed the mud from its wheels and did not leave it until it was in perfect order and ready to go out at once on parade should occasion require it.

Baron Bernstoff viewed all these details with interest and approval, for the care with which everything was attended to and the industry with which the men went about their duties appealed strongly to his German mind, while his English friend, although he watched everything just as attentively, did not seem nearly so much impressed with what he saw and was evidently very skeptical in regard to the efficiency of the American service. It was plain enough to Chief Trask, who was a keenly observant man, that in his secret heart the Honorable Rupert Doubter was not quite willing to trust the evidence of his own eyes and regarded all that he saw as things done simply for show and not for use.

"That's all very well," he said at last, "and it seems to me that if you could tell exactly when a fire was going to break out your service would be perfect, but supposing the alarm comes in when some of the men are playing checkers and others are up stairs taking a nap, and a few more perhaps are up at the corner——"

But here the chief interrupted him rather sharply. "My men don't spend their time hanging round street corners, and they don't take naps in the afternoon like a lot of old maids. They play checkers sometimes, but I can tell you that if that gong rings they stop just where they are and don't wait to finish the game. As I told you before our motto is to be always ready and I've forgotten the Latin words for it, I am sorry to say. The alarm may come in in the middle of the night when they're all in bed and asleep, and it may come in and find them all down stairs as you see them now, but the result is the same. By the time the driver gets into his seat the men are on the truck behind him, and off they go. If you will come upstairs with me I'll take pleasure in showing you where we sleep and the way we have of getting out on time when we're sent for."

Saying this, Chief Trask escorted his visitors up stairs to the dormitory, where he explained the method of turning out at night and sliding down the brass poles. To illustrate the last named feat, he called Bruce upstairs and had him go through the act of jumping against the pole and sliding down it to the floor below. The foreigners witnessed the act in silent amazement, and then the Englishman turned to Chief Trask and said, "Upon me soul, this is all very extraordinary, don't you know, but I would like to ask why they don't go down the staircase; it must be so much easier, and it is certainly not so wearing on their clothes,"

"The staircase!" cried Chief Trask, in horror, "Why, that would take them fully five seconds longer than it does this way."

"But what does five seconds count in getting to a fire?" persisted Mr. Doubter.

"I can tell you, sir," replied the chief, "that we look upon five seconds as a considerable period of time in the matter of getting out to answer an alarm."

The Englishman shrugged his shoulders and said nothing further, and a moment or two later Mr. Dewsnap took the chief one side and whispered to him that he was sure Mr. Doubter did not believe one word that was said to him, and as for Baron Bernstoff, he was so accustomed to the old fashioned, slow-but-sure methods in vogue in his native land, that it was impossible to convince him that in a fire brigade, if nowhere else, quickness was an indispensable quality.

"Why," exclaimed the enthusiastic old gentleman, "I told these men again and again about the time it takes to get out into the street and get a stream on at a fire, but it's impossible to convince them, and if you were to hear them talk about the way they run these things on the other side, you would know why it is that they can't comprehend our methods."

"And do you mean to tell me," inquired the German baron, "that when an alarm comes in, let us say at midnight, your men jump right out of their beds, slide down those poles, and get away to the fire all in the space of a few minutes and without leaving anyone behind?"

"In a few minutes!" cried the chief, contemptuously, "why how long do you imagine that it takes us to get up and get dressed, hitch up the horses and get started?"

The foreigners immediately began to calculate on their fingers. "To begin with," said Baron Bernstoff, "I suppose that the light sleepers wake up of their own accord, and then go around and arouse such of their comrades as have not heard the alarm. That must take a minute and a half at the very least."

The chief's eyes twinkled with amusement, and one of the men, who had been standing within earshot, walked hurriedly to the window for fear that his desire to laugh would get the better of him. Bruce, though he felt the same inclination, managed to control his features out of respect to the chief and his visitors, but Mr. Dewsnap had no such scruples, and he uttered a whoop of merriment which was contagious enough to cause the chief, Bruce, and even the fireman at the window to break out into sudden peals of mirth.

"Go on sir?" said the chief apologetically, "It only seemed funny to us because such a thing as a man being a light sleeper is unheard of in the department. There's no time allowed for him to sit up in bed and stretch himself and yawn and maybe ask somebody what time it is. He's expected to jump out of bed and land on his feet in his turnout at the very first stroke of the gong, even if he happens to be dreaming that he is Chief of the whole New York Fire Department. Well according to your calculations we'll make it a minute and a half to get waked up. Now go on."

"Then," continued the Baron, "I don't suppose that a man is expected to make a very elaborate toilet even if he is going out into the streets, but he must put on his clothes, wash his hands and face——"

"We're apt to get all the drenching we want when we get to the fire," interjected Chief Trask, and the Baron continued without seeming to comprehend his remarks, "Well, suppose we say three minutes for dressing and another minute to get down stairs and hitch the horses—you don't stop to call the roll of the men, do you?"

"No," rejoined the chief gravely "our only roll is the pay roll and a man drops off that pretty quick if he's not at his place when the truck goes out."

"Let me see," continued the visitor, "that makes five minutes and a half so far. If you get out in six minutes, you ought to do well. But there's one thing I don't understand and that is how you can be sure of arriving at the fire with the full strength of your company if you don't call the roll or have some other means of assuring yourself that they're all there when you started. Now in my country the men all stand up in a row and are inspected by their commanding officer before they leave their quarters, and each one must have his boots blacked and his clothing all properly arranged before he gets up on the engine."

"If we were to stop here to inspect our men we'd never get to the fire at all," replied the chief. "If a man doesn't take interest enough in his work to turn out the instant the alarm comes, why there's no room for him in the department. Why, the rivalry between the different companies is so strong that every fireman feels that the reputation of his own machine rests on his shoulders, and, as I told you before, when that alarm comes in he gives a jump, no matter whether he is asleep or in the middle of a game of checkers——"

"Would he jump if he were in the middle of a game of pinochle," interrupted the Baron with a look of inquiring gravity that almost upset Mr. Dewsnap again.

"He'd jump no matter what he was doing," the chief went on "and as for six minutes—well come down stairs with me, and I'll turn the men out for your especial benefit, then you can take your watch out and time them so as to see just how long it does take."

Followed by the two foreigners and their American friend, Chief Trask proceeded down the stairs while Bruce descended by the more convenient and speedy pole. "You'd better come out here on the sidewalk where you won't be in the way of the horses," he remarked, and then, just as Baron Bernstoff had taken his watch from his pocket, the quick sharp notes of the gong fell upon their ears. It was a real alarm that had come in this time and the astounded foreigners saw the horses spring to their places and the driver climb to the seat, while the chief bounded into his wagon. Then the harness was fastened on both vehicles with a succession of sharp clicks. Charley Weyman, whose practiced eye had already told him that everything was securely fastened, detached the reins from the ceiling with a sudden pull and the next moment the big truck with Brophy at the wheel swept out of the quarters, just as the chief's wagon dashed through the other door, turned sharply to the right, knocking the Honorable Rupert Doubter over on his back as it went by, and was nearly at the corner of the street when the Englishman picked himself up from the gutter and said to his friend.

"Did you get the beggars' time?"

"I forgot all about it," rejoined the other with a sheepish glance at his watch, "but it's just ten seconds now so they must have got off in about six."

"Ten seconds!" cried Mr. Doubter, true to his convictions to the very last, "Why your watch must have stopped, man. I've been lying on my back in the road there nearly five minutes I am sure. But what's become of our friend Dewsnap?"

"He's gone to the fire," replied the Baron. "I saw him waving his hand to us as he went by."

It was indeed true, Mr. Dewsnap, the most confirmed fire crank in New York, had mounted the truck along with the men and dashed off to the scene of action, leaving his two friends to shift for themselves.

"Did you get the beggars' time?"—*Page 136.*

Chapter XVI.

THERE came a time when Chief Trask began to entertain doubts in regard to his young protege. He noticed that Bruce was growing absent-minded and seemed to have lost, if not interest in his work, at least a great deal of the enthusiasm which he had shown during his first weeks at the quarters. The boy would stand in the doorway, leaning on the chains, for an hour at a time, gazing vacantly into the street, and when called he would respond in an indolent, careless fashion, which was very different from the quick way which had previously characterized him. The chief watched him narrowly these days, and often asked himself if it were possible that he could be to blame for Bruce's retrogression.

"It may be," he said to himself one day, "that the boy has not enough to do, and is getting discontented because he finds the work so monotonous. It's a queer sort of position for a lad to find himself in anyway, for at present he's neither fish, flesh, fowl, nor good red herring. If he were a little older I'd try to get him a regular appointment in the department, but, as it is, I don't see that I can do anything more for him except, maybe, to let him go to a fire now and then. It would be good practice for him and give him something new to think about."

Bruce was growing discontented, there was no doubt about that. The work, although not severe, was monotonous, and he found the confinement at the quarters, especially while the men were away at fires, extremely irksome. Moreover, he noticed that other lads of his age who were employed in mercantile houses seemed to live more active lives, to make fairly good wages, and to have altogether a better time than he did. He had pictured the life in the fire department as one of brilliant excitement, highly spiced with adventure and danger; and he had fancied himself as a sort of hero in a blue uniform and with a big fireman's hat on his head, dashing through the streets on a fire engine or rescuing people from burning houses. He had also dreamt of getting his name, and perhaps his picture, into the newspapers, and of rising so rapidly in the department as to become its chief by the time he was twenty-one. And now instead of this life of adventure and success he found himself cooped up in a truck company's quarters all day long with very little to do but look after the horses, help the men about the truck and run errands for the chief of battalion. These duties were certainly not exhilarating, and he had already become very tired of them, but it was positively galling to be compelled to stay behind when the company went to fires, and he never saw them set out without gazing longingly after the truck and wishing that he were riding on it at the side of Tom Brophy.

But there are little things which change the current of human life, and one of these little things happened just as Bruce was on the point of asking the chief to let him take a position in some store or office and give up the fire department altogether. One afternoon, having been given a leave of absence from the quarters, he strolled down to Captain Murphy's engine house, in order to have a chat with the captain, who had taken quite a liking to the son of his old friend and was always delighted to talk to him about the work in the department and to explain things that he did not know.

"They ought to take you with them to fires," said the captain after he had finished some trivial detail which the boy did not understand.

"I'd like nothing better than to go to fires all the time," replied Bruce, "but the fact is that the chief wants me to stay at the quarters while the men are away. So, while they're off fighting the fire, I have to hang around and wait for them to come back. It's mighty stupid work I can tell you, and I don't mind saying that I'm getting rather sick of it and would like to find a job somewhere else."

"I guess that's what's the matter with you, young man," replied the captain. "You don't get variety enough in your life, and the next time I see the chief, I'm going to speak to him about it. You'll never fit yourself to take a good position in the department unless you go out with the men. You can learn more by helping to put out one fire than you can by sitting around an engine house for a year. You'd better not think of looking for another job though, until you give this business a fair trial. There's no reason why you shouldn't make as good a fireman as your father was, for you're quick and you've got a cool head on you just like that bay horse over there. There are some boys that you could never make firemen of, because they're lazy and will shirk their work whenever they can, just like that black horse that goes on the tender. We've had him here a week and he's going back to-morrow because he is no good " Bruce looked at the two animals as the captain pointed them out to him, and realized that there was as much variety in horses as in boys. The bay who helped to pull the fire engine was a strong, clean limbed animal with a fine shaped head, sensitive ears and a quick, alert look in his face that was unmistakeable. The black, on the other hand, was a fat, sleepy looking animal who held his head down most of the time, and had such thick, clumsy looking legs that Bruce wondered how it was that he ever got to a fire on time.

"The next time—" began Captain Murphy, but what he intended to say will never be known, for just at that moment the sharp stroke of the gong startled him to his feet. Bruce started also, from mere force of habit, little dreaming of the whole significance of that sharply clanging bell. From force of habit also he turned to see if he couldn't lend a hand. The men were already at the heads of the engine horses, and the heavy footed black was lumbering slowly from his stall to his place at the pole of the tender.

Without waiting to be told, Bruce sprang at his head, snapped the collar about his neck, adjusted his head-stall and attached the reins, and did it all so quickly and thoroughly that Captain Murphy, who was just leaping from the floor to his place on the ash-pan, cried out: "Well done, young man, we'll make a fireman of you yet."

And then, acting on the spur of a sudden and fortunate inspiration, Bruce made answer, with a meaning glance at his superior: "Not unless you give me a chance to go to fires."

"Up with you, then," rejoined the captain, and the boy sprang up beside him just as the engine started. As they passed across the threshold the engineer lit his torch of oil-soaked rags and threw it under the boiler, which was filled with kindling wood also soaked in oil. The flames blazed up fiercely, fanned by the draft made by the swift motion of the vehicle, and in a moment the engineer was feeding them with one shovel after another of coal. By this time the engine was racing madly up the street, ringing its brass bell in sharp warning to all in its course. Captain Murphy was standing on the ash-pan, peering anxiously ahead of him, while Bruce stood beside him, keeping his place as best he could and wondering if it could be possible that the horses were running away. Just behind them came the tender, the black horse and his gray mate going at full gallop and following in the trail of glowing cinders which marked the engine's course. Drivers and foot passengers hastened to make way for the firemen, so that they reached Fifth avenue with hardly a second's loss of time. But just before they turned into the great thoroughfare the noise of another bell fell upon Bruce's ears, and, with a roar and a rush, another engine with its tender close behind dashed up the avenue just ahead of them followed by a trail of smoke and red cinders.

"Just our luck!" exclaimed Captain Murphy, as he stamped his foot impatiently, for it was the rival company which had passed them half a block ahead, and as it went by Bruce noticed that Captain Baker, who was standing on the ash-pan, waved his hand in ironical salute to Captain Murphy.

"That's the second time they've got ahead of us in a month," continued Captain Murphy, "and now they'll get first water, for I'm afraid we'll never be able to catch them."

Then the captain shouted some unintelligible order to his driver, who was urging his horses to even greater speed than before, in an attempt to pass the other machine. Standing on tiptoe and looking ahead it seemed to Bruce that they were slowly gaining on their rival, and that if the race were long enough they would inevitably catch up with it. But they were drawing near to the scene of the fire, and, with a sharp whirl, the foremost engine turned from the broad avenue into a side street.

"Hold fast!" shouted Captain Murphy, as his engine went round the corner in a way that nearly threw Bruce off his feet, and then, without an instant's delay, swept on in mad pursuit of the other. Far ahead, the crowd could be seen gathering in the roadway close to a building from which a thick column of smoke was ascending to the sky. Captain Baker's engine still maintained the lead, and it was plain that unless something remarkable happened, she would have her stream on the fire first.

But remarkable things sometimes do happen in real life, and now, just as both engines were slowing down, while their captains looked anxiously about them as if in search of something, Bruce saw a grin of delight chase the clouds from Captain Murphy's face, and then a sharp word of command caused the driver to come to a sudden stop close to the curb, and there stood Mr. Peter Dewsnap leaning carelessly on an ash barrel and waving his hand to Captain Murphy. In an instant the barrel was lifted from the sidewalk and hurled into the street, and then Bruce saw to his surprise that it had been placed over the hydrant for which both captains were looking, and all at once he realized that Mr. Dewsnap, who was a particular friend of Captain Murphy's, had placed it there and mounted guard over it in order to prevent the other company from getting their stream on first. Captain Baker saw through the game, but just too late, for before he could reach the spot the engineer had his coupling attached and the men were beginning to stretch hose.

"You stay with the tender until I send for you!" cried Captain Murphy, as he disappeared through the crowd.

Chapter XVII.

IT was the first dangerous fire that Bruce had ever witnessed, and, having tied the horses to a convenient tree, he climbed up on the tender in order to get a good view of what was going on.

A slight blaze had started in some cotton waste in a five-story brick building used for manufacturing purposes, and by the time the firemen arrived the smoke was pouring out of the upper windows in dense clouds, while the workmen and women were escaping, bareheaded, to the street, many of them coming through the big door on the ground floor, while others, in their anxiety to save themselves, came crashing through the lower windows and jumped to the sidewalk, heedless of the flying splinters of glass. The fire-escape, a series of iron balconies connected by ladders, was by this time crowded with frightened women making the best of their way to the ground, and it seemed to Bruce's excited mind that the whole building must be full of human beings and that many of them would inevitably perish before aid could reach them.

By this time half a dozen policemen, who had been summoned by the alarm, had driven back the rapidly gathering crowd and established "fire lines" about the burning building. Chief Trask had assumed command of all the operations, and the men were working rapidly and effectively under his orders. Familiar as he was with the quick methods of the department, Bruce was surprised to see what progress had been made while he was tying his horses and climbing up into the driver's seat of the tender. The engine company had already connected their hose, stretched a suitable length of line and attached a brass pipe to the end of it, while the men from the truck had placed a tall ladder against the building and were preparing to ascend it. The other engine had also made connection with a hydrant around the corner, and the noise that the two machines made was audible over everything else. And now Captain Murphy gave the word of command to his men and, with the pipe in his hand, entered the building, the others following, carrying the hose in their arms, each man about twenty-five feet—half the distance between the joints—from the one behind him. Bruce saw that Tom Brophy was half way up the tall ladder and was shouting to a woman who clung, nearly crazed with fright, to a window on the fourth floor.

"Stay where you are!" yelled the fireman, and the woman had just sense and strength enough left to obey. Bruce watched him as he moved up the ladder. It seemed to him fully five minutes before he reached her, although in reality it was not more than five seconds. There was another delay then which seemed interminable to the excited boy, for the fireman before lifting the woman from her perilous position stopped to attach a snap hook which hung from a band about his waist to the rung of the ladder. This done, and having both arms free, he reached forward and lifted her in his strong arms. Bruce heard what sounded like a loud sigh of relief, and glancing up he found that it came from the lips of the people who were hanging out of every window that commanded a sight of the fire; they had watched the unfortunate working woman as she clung to the window, and it was with heartfelt relief that they saw her safe in Brophy's arms. Bruce, too, felt a strange choking in his throat, and knew that the tears were beginning to trickle down his cheek. He was glad that neither Chief Trask nor Captain Murphy could see him then, for he felt ashamed of his weakness.

Meantime, there arose before him what looked like the Eiffel Tower on a small scale; it was surmounted by a pipe with a curved end, and as he looked a stream of water burst from the pipe and fell against the wall of the building. Then the pipe moved slowly until it discharged its stream directly into an open window, and Bruce saw that it was worked by means of a lever at its base, and that one of the men from the quarters was moving it. Not until that moment did he realize that what he saw was the water-tower which had been swiftly and silently erected and put in operation. Then other engines with their hose tenders came thundering down the street, for Mr. Trask had already rung a second alarm in view of the fact that the fire was likely to prove a dangerous one and difficult to handle. There was another battalion chief on the ground also, but although Bruce knew that he was Mr. Trask's senior in rank and years of service, he did not assume the command and for two reasons: the fire lay within the junior chief's district, and besides the latter had been the first on the scene of action.

And while all this had been going on about him, Bruce noted everything that he saw from his seat on the tender, and wished that he, too, might do his share in the work of fighting the flames. So much had been accomplished before his eyes that he could hardly believe it possible that but a very few minutes had elapsed since his arrival on the ground. A familiar voice greeted him, and looking down he saw Mr. Peter Dewsnap standing on the sidewalk beside the tender, and wiping the perspiration from his flushed face.

"So they are going to make a regular fireman of you," remarked the old gentleman, pleasantly.

"I hope so," replied the boy, as he descended from his perch. "This is the first big blaze I've seen since I came to New York. I noticed you standing beside that ash barrel when I came along."

"Yes," replied Mr. Dewsnap, "that's an old trick of the Volunteer Department. You see Captain Murphy's a particular friend of mine, and when I saw the smoke I knew he would have hard work to get his stream on first, for the other house is nearer by half a block, so I just grabbed an ash barrel, dumped the ashes into the street, and clapped it over the hydrant; that's the reason that other company passed it, and Murphy's men got their connection made first. But I'm afraid this is going to be a very hot blaze, my boy, and they tell me they haven't got all the people out of the building yet."

And as he spoke the flames burst out from every window on the fourth floor and the heat became so intense that the people in the windows across the street drew back, while the firemen pulled their hats down over their faces and one or two of them deliberately soaked themselves with water from the hose. All this time streams of water from the water-tower and the different lines of hose had fallen upon the flames without making any apparent effect; Bruce knew that Captain Murphy was somewhere inside the burning building with his men and he wondered fearfully if they would ever come out alive. They were paying out more hose near him, and he saw what he recognized as a siamese connection brought from one of the tenders and attached to a rubber hose of more than ordinary thickness. Bruce knew what the connection was used for, and in company with Mr. Dewsnap, who knew almost as much about it as the men themselves, he crossed the street and watched the men as they attached to the joint two separate lines of hose, each one of which was connected with an engine. Then the signal was given and two streams of water were forced, each by its own engine, through the brass connection, or siamese joint, and into the big hose, forming one stream of tremendous power. When this stream was turned on the building its effect on the flames was apparent at once.

And now there were other people besides the firemen and Mr. Dewsnap walking about inside the fire lines and stepping over the lengths of black hose, which were curling and writhing about the street like so many big serpents. Standing near the corner, Bruce noticed half a dozen well dressed young men, who were watching the scene carefully and from time to time making notes in books which they took from their pockets. They were the reporters of the daily newspapers who had been sent to the scene of action as soon as the alarm came in. Each one wore on his breast a silver plated fire-badge, issued by the department, which gave him the right to cross the line. Another man who wore a similar badge and stood in earnest conversation with the chief, was, so Mr. Dewsnap said, an employee of one of the great electric companies.

"And very useful those electric men are at a fire sometimes," explained the old gentleman. "You see these electric wires were unknown in my time, but now it is a very important matter to keep track of them at a fire because it is a dangerous thing to have them break loose and swing about while the men are at work. It's death to put your finger on one of them; and there's no one but a regular employee of one of the electric companies that can handle them with any safety. Then there's that chap from the gas works; he has a badge because he's a useful man, too. Sometimes a stream of water thrown into a room will break a chandelier short off and then the gas escapes and there is liable to be an explosion when the flames reach it."

"You're wanted, Bruce!" cried a grimy fireman, as he rushed up to where the boy was standing.

The boy's eyes flashed, and then he said reluctantly; "But Captain Murphy told me to watch the horses."

"You go along!" exclaimed Mr. Dewsnap, peremptorily, "I'll stay by the tender until you come back," and the boy darted off without waiting to thank him.

Captain Murphy's company was short handed and Bruce was wanted to take a length of the hose. The captain was just entering the building by means of a ladder which reached to the third floor, and Bruce, taking his place on the hose, followed upwards the last of the line of men. The window at which the captain was making his entrance had received but five minutes before the thick stream of water directed by two fire engines through the siamese joint and when they stepped over the charred and smoking window-sill they found the room black with smoke, and fully six inches of water on the floor. It was a hard pull to get the heavy hose up the ladder but Bruce did his best with the men and followed them as they climbed through the window. As the water surged about his feet he looked at the darkness before him and admitted to himself that he would not have dared to enter that building unless the others had gone before him. But no thought of turning back entered the boy's mind. Not for any reward on earth would he have dropped his hose and sneaked back down the ladder. The smoke closed around him and made his eyes smart so that he could not keep them open; but still he kept on, unable to see the man who was twenty-five feet in front of him, but knowing by the drag on the hose that he was there. Where the captain was leading him or for what purpose he did not know. He was simply a soldier obeying orders. And the feeling that he was at last doing something as a fireman came upon him with a keen sense of exhilaration.

On they went through smoke and water. Every moment Bruce stumbled over some box or piece of furniture and once he fell full length on the floor; but he picked himself up, seized the hose, and blindly followed as it drew him across the room. He stumbled again, but this time it was not a box or a piece of furniture that his foot encountered but something that yielded as he touched it, and suggested somehow the horrible idea that it was a dead human body. Stooping down and groping with his hands he touched a warm human face; and then, still groping and feeling with his hands, he found that it was the body of a boy who had evidently been smothered in smoke. For a moment Bruce stood undecided as to what course he should pursue. The hose was still traveling across the floor, at a rapid rate, and although he shouted to his companions he could hear nothing in reply. Should he follow them as had been ordered or should he turn back with the boy's body in his arms? All at once he remembered that Mr. Trask had once told him that a fireman's first duty was to save human life—and saying to himself "I'll be on the safe side anyhow," he lifted the inanimate form in his arms and slowly made his way back to the window by which he had entered.

So quiet was his burden that he felt sure there was no more life in the frail body, but no sooner had he gained the fresh air, than the lips began to move, and a feeble movement of the arms told him that his efforts had not been in vain. Fortunately his burden was but a light one, and wrapping one arm tightly about it he managed to climb out on the ladder and carry it down to the street. Then without an instant's hesitation he climbed up the ladder again and began to follow the line of hose, which was still moving as swiftly as before. But he had not gone far before a great flash of light lit up the room in which he was, and then it seemed to him as if the building shook beneath his feet. Looking behind him he saw a great wall of solid flame rise up from the floor. The hose was still moving through his hand, and with one look behind, he plunged bravely into the dark smoke that lay before him.

"He managed to climb out on the ladder and carry it down to the street."—*Page 156*.

Chapter XVIII.

BRUCE DECKER was grit clear through, but all at once there came into his mind the thought of his father and of the great fire in which he had lost his life. He had gone in among the smoke and the flame on that fateful day with a length of hose under his arm, and he had never come out. For one brief moment his son wondered if he too were doomed to perish in a like manner. Then, by a strong effort of will, he drove the thought from his mind, and the bright face of Laura Van Kuren came up before him and nerved him to do his best.

Taking a tight grip on the hose, which quivered like a thing of life as the swift stream of water rushed through it, the boy stumbled blindly on through the heavy smoke. He could see nothing, for, with his lack of experience, he did not know, as the older firemen did, how to protect his eyes. He had lost his cap, too, and a hot cinder falling on his head made him wish that he had on one of the heavy fireman's caps which he used to think so cumbrous. He made no pretense of dragging the hose now. It was dragging him, and he had not gone far before he was thrown with sudden force against some obstruction, and fell at full length on a narrow flight of stairs. As he struggled to his feet he heard the hoarse word of command somewhere above him, and the hose came to a standstill. The men had made their way through the room and upstairs to the floor above. He could hear them plainly, tramping about and shouting in the darkness. He could hear the hissing of the flames, too, as the water fell upon them, and already there was a thick stream flowing in a series of miniature cascades down the narrow flight of steps.

There was nothing for him to do now but follow on, until he reached his old place twenty-five feet behind the man in front of him, and so he groped his way up the steps, and crawling on all fours with the hose under him, followed the long, black, quivering trail until he could see dimly the forms of the other men. Then he stopped, and, not knowing what else to do, lifted the line from the floor, and stood with it under his arm awaiting further orders.

By this time the well directed streams from without and within the building had had their effect on the flames, and a strong wind, entering through the windows which had been broken by the firemen, was driving out the black clouds of smoke, and leaving a purer and clearer atmosphere in their stead. This enabled him to see the group of men who stood about twenty feet in front of him, with the captain among them, and the water still rushing from the brass pipe which he held in his hand. Then there was another sharp order, the captain moved on and the men, gathering up the slack hose, followed in a long line as before, with Bruce at the rear. Through an open window they went, one after another, still carrying the hose, and dropping on a tin roof beneath them.

"Let the last man stand in the window and look out for the hose!" was the order given in stentorian tones that reached Bruce's ear as the men climbed, one after another, into a window that opened out on a roof just opposite him.

"Aye, aye, sir," he shouted in reply, as he took up his position just inside the open window, and, by the exercise of every particle of his strength, managed to keep the hose from being injured by nails or sudden jets of flames as it was dragged rapidly across the sill. He saw the other men appear at a window above the one they had entered, and lift the hose up to it by means of a piece of rope. Then they disappeared, the hose moving after them for a few minutes, when it stopped and remained suspended from one window to the other about six feet above the low tin roof over which the captain and his men had passed.

Then, for the first time since the Captain had thundered back his order, Bruce looked about him and was dimayed to find the smoke pouring up the staircase in much denser and blacker clouds than before, filling the room so as to completely shut out every thing from his sight, and pouring out of the upper part of the window by which he stood, in a dark stream, which was growing thicker and darker every moment. A little gust of wind swept some of the smoke into his face and made him turn, gasping and with smarting eyes, to the fresh air.

Leaning far out across the window ledge, he gazed at the opposite window to which the hose led, and called aloud to Captain Murphy. But no reply was wafted back to him from the smoke and the flames, and the horrible thought came across him that perhaps his mates had forgotten him. But with characteristic pluck and self-reliance, he fought back the idea before it had fairly taken lodgment in his brain, and turned his attention to making a careful survey of his surroundings. Behind him was a great room that was so filled with a dense, black smoke that it would be impossible, if the worst came to the worst, for him to cross it and make his way down the narrow staircase. And even if he did find the staircase and descended in safety, what would he find at the foot of it? He was likely to find the lower floors all ablaze and ready to collapse as he walked across them. Then he looked down at the tin roof beneath the window, and saw that in two or three places the metal had melted, and thin jets of flame were beginning to burst through.

That his life was in extreme peril he could no longer doubt, and that there was still a chance of saving it by deserting his post he well knew. He could leap down, make a dash for it across the roof and through the window and easily find the others by simply following the line of the hose, and for a moment he stood irresolutely with one leg thrown across the ledge and the other foot resting across the floor. But he did not hesitate long; he had been told to remain at the window, and what would Captain Murphy and Chief Trask think of a boy who had lost his head and disobeyed orders the very first time he was assigned to an important and dangerous duty? It might be, after all, that the danger was not as great as he imagined, and he comforted himself with that assurance, at the same time carefully nourishing his faith in Captain Murphy, who would not, he was positive, go off and leave his youngest subordinate to face death alone.

There was nothing dramatic or imaginative about the hero of this story; he was simply a plain, straightforward, courageous American boy, who could always be depended upon to act rather than to talk or pose. And in this moment of supreme danger it did not occur to him that his position between the black smoke that was rolling up behind him and the red flames that were bursting out before and under his very eyes, was an unusual or heroic one. It had been his ambition ever since his arrival in New York to take an active part in the work of the fire department, and now for the first time he had realized his ambition and had an opportunity, if not to distinguish himself, at least to show what sort of stuff he was made of.

It was an opportunity in which he gloried, with a sense of exaltation such as he had seldom known in the whole course of his life, and he resolved then and there that neither smoke nor flames should drive him from his post unless he first received orders from his superior officers.

And it happened that just as he uttered this resolution to himself Captain Murphy, working with his men in the other building to which the hose was stretched, exclaimed: "What's become of that boy Decker? Has anything happened to him?"

Then he remembered that he himself had ordered Bruce to remain at the window, and knowing the lad's firmness of character and tenacity, the thought occurred to him that possibly he was still there, waiting further orders, although when he gave his command he had only intended to have him remain there so long as the line was moving. Handing the brass pipe to one of his men the captain dashed across the floor, looked through the window and saw Bruce with his jacket tied around his head, lying with his body stretched half way across the sill.

"Come over here quick!" he yelled, and Bruce, only too glad to obey, leaped down to the roof and started across. But to his horror he felt the hot metal sagging beneath his feet like thin ice after a February thaw. The flames were bursting out in a dozen places, and by this time the captain realized the danger and called to him to make haste. Above his head swung the hose, and ten feet further, provided the roof held up, would bring him to a point where it sagged so low as to be within his reach. He was just in time, for as he caught it a great sheet of flame burst up in exactly the place across which he had passed, and then a portion of the roof went down in front of him and a cloud of smoke and cinders, interspersed with darting tongues of flame, rose up and shut out Captain Murphy from his sight.

With the agility of a cat the boy swung himself up on the line, wound his jacket still more closely about his head, and, encouraged by the shouts of the officer whom he could no longer see, started to crawl along his frail bridge through the thick curtain of smoke and fire. The heat was awful, his clothing was afire in half a dozen places, and he knew that the hose could not hold out much longer against the flames. At one time it seemed as if he could go no further, but must let go and drop into the fiery chasm beneath him. Then by a final effort he called to his aid all his reserve force of courage, obstinacy and determination, crawled blindly along the line, found himself in a clearer and cooler air, heard the captain's voice close to him, and then a strong hand clutched him by the shoulder and dragged him through the window.

And just at that moment the hose yielded to the intense heat and burst, discharging a stream of water into the flames beneath. The end to which Bruce still clung as the captain dragged him through the window hung down like a lifeless thing, but the other end was thrashing about like a wounded serpent, and hurling thick streams of water in every direction.

Once inside the window the boy collapsed altogether and fell upon the floor, but Captain Murphy lifted him up as if he had been a baby and bore him rapidly to a window on the other side of the building from which he took him, by means of a thirty-five foot ladder, to the street below, placed him tenderly on the sidewalk, and then returned to his post as a familiar voice exclaimed: "I'll look after the lad."

It was Peter Dewsnap who bent down over the blackened and apparently lifeless form of the boy as he lay on the pavement, and, as the old gentleman raised his head after listening a moment at the lad's left side, he said:

"Thank God, he is alive, but there's no telling how badly he's hurt. Have you rung for an ambulance?"

Yes, that had been done already, and in a few minutes the vehicle, with its uniformed driver and surgeon and its sharp clanging bell, was making its way through the crowd, which by this time had reached enormous proportions. It drew up near the curbstone, the surgeon leaped to the ground and knelt down beside the unconscious boy. Mr. Dewsnap was sitting in the gutter beside him, regardless of his fine clothes, and briskly rubbing his hands in the hope of restoring the circulation. Chief Trask, who had lingered a moment to assure himself that the lad was still alive, had returned to his duties, but the reporters had gathered about and, in a quick, business-like way, were questioning Mr. Dewsnap and the surgeon.

"Does anybody know the boy's name or how he happened to get hurt?" asked a pleasant faced young chap, who had a note-book and pencil in his hand.

"Bruce Decker is his name," replied the old gentleman, "and he's not regularly in the department but helps the chief down at headquarters. Why, his father was killed in that Broadway apartment house fire some time ago."

"I remember all about it," rejoined the young man, and then turning to his companions, he said: "Don't you remember that Frank Decker, the fireman who was lost when that apartment house burned down? I covered that fire and I remember all about it."

"Just give me a hand, will you, I think I'll take this young man right up to the hospital," said the surgeon, who had been making a superficial examination of Bruce's injuries. "I took a young kid up there from this very fire half an hour ago."

Then, with Mr. Dewsnap's assistance, he deposited Bruce on the spring mattress inside the ambulance, resumed his seat behind him and told the driver to go on.

Mr. Dewsnap stood watching the departing vehicle with an anxious, troubled face and then, turning to the reporter with whom he had spoken before, he said: "That young lad whom they have just carried off is the worthy son of a good father, and if it hadn't been for him, that other boy that the surgeon spoke of wouldn't have been saved. He found him lying on the floor up there, and I myself saw him carry him down the ladder and then go right back to his work again. That's a pretty good record for a boy to make at his first fire, isn't it."

The reporters listened attentively to what Mr. Dewsnap said, and made frequent entries in their note-books. Most of them knew the old gentleman as a fire-crank, frequently encountered at fires, and one who was always ready to furnish them with any information they required. It was he to whom they usually went if any one was hurt, for he knew the names and histories of all the important men in the department as well as those of the subordinate firemen employed in Chief Trask's battalion, in which he claimed a sort of honorary membership.

Chapter XIX.

BRUCE awoke at a very early hour in the morning and found himself in a clean, white, comfortable bed, which was not his own. His eyes were dim and there was a soreness in his lungs when he tried to breathe. He was conscious, moreover, of dull pains in his arms and legs, and he felt as weak as if he had just recovered from a long fit of illness. He did not know where he was and he did not care, his only wish being to lie perfectly quiet and if possible to go to sleep sgain. He closed his eyes for a moment or two and then his natural instincts seemed to return, so he opened them again and stared curiously about him. He was in a long, high room, with plenty of light and air in it and a row of tall windows stretching along one side of it. There were other cots similar to his own in the room, and each one had its occupant.

For some time he rested quietly on his back, moving his head slightly, from time to time, in order to see everything in the room and wondering the while, whether he were asleep or awake. Then an indistinct remembrance of the exciting events of the day before returned to him, and it seemed as if he were still breathing the hot smoke which had filled the burning building.

"How do you feel this morning?"

These words were uttered in a soft, womanly voice, and on turning his head, he saw standing by his bedside one of the prettiest young ladies he had ever seen. Her dress was of a quiet Scotch plaid, and she wore over her dark hair a most becoming little white cap, of a style that was perfectly new to him.

"I feel queer," was his simple answer and then he asked, with a faint show of interest: "How did I get here, and where am I?"

"You're in good hands and you'll soon be well again, Bruce, but you must be careful not to move about too much in your bed or to worry yourself unnecessarily," was the young lady's reply, but although it was uttered in the gentlest and most reassuring tones, he could not help noticing its evasive nature, so he repeated his question, "Where am I?"

"You're in an hospital, and you must stay here until you are well enough to go out again," said the young lady, and then as she saw a look of dismay coming to the boy's face, she continued, "But you needn't be afraid, for it is a very nice hospital, indeed, and you will have everything that is good for you, and I am sure that you will get well very fast. Now shut your eyes again and try to go to sleep, and by and by I will bring you some breakfast."

The young lady with the white cap inspired so much confidence in the young boy that he dismissed all anxiety and curiosity from his mind, closed his eyes and was soon in a deep sleep, from which he did not awaken until nearly all the rest of the sleepers in the big room were either sitting up in bed or dressed and walking about. He felt much more refreshed now, and as he stared about him, he wondered what had become of the young lady, and how soon she would bring his breakfast to him.

"Hay, boss, wot place is dis?" said a piping voice close beside him, and as Bruce turned his head, he saw in the cot next to his a face that seemed familiar, and was connected in his mind in some way with the fire and smoke and excitement of the day before. It was the face of a boy, and a very homely little boy at that. It was a boy with a freckled face, turned up nose, and a pair of sharp, small, blue eyes, which looked at him from under a thick mat of coarse red hair which hung down over his forehead in rebellious locks, and added measurably to the foxy expression of his face.

"Who are you, anyhow?" demanded Bruce.

"I'm Skinny de Swiper, an' I'd like ter know wot dey brung me here fer."

"I'm sure I don't know," said the other, and then he added with a smile "I don't even know what I'm doing here myself, but where do you come from? Where do you live when you're home?"

"Sometimes one place, and sometimes anudder; last week I got a job in a factory over in 18th Street, but dere was a fire dere, an' I guess I muster got burned up. I kin just remember a bloke collarin' me an' and trowin' me down a ladder; he muster been a fireman."

The boy's simple explanation cleared some of the cobwebs out of Bruce's mind, and he suddenly recalled his entrance, with the hose under his arm, into the burning building and the boy whom he had dragged through the window and down the ladder to the street. "I guess," he remarked, "that I'm the bloke that carried you out."

"Come off!" said the boy in a tone of mingled scorn and incredulity, "dere ain't no kids like you in de fire department, an' I guess I'd oughter know."

"Very well then," replied Bruce, annoyed at the other's contemptuous words, "maybe I'm not in the department, but I helped to put that fire out all the same. If I hadn't I wouldn't be here now."

He would have said more if he had not been interrupted by the young lady with the white cap, who came up to him at this moment in company with another young lady dressed exactly like herself and with the same gentle manner and soft voice. The second young lady was the day-nurse and the other nurse was telling her about the cases that had been brought into the ward during the night. In a few words she explained the injuries which the two boys were suffering from and then asked them if they would like something to eat. They were both hungry and in a few minutes a tray with coffee, toast, and an egg was placed on each bed. Skinny ate his breakfast without any assistance, but Bruce had to be helped by the day-nurse, a process which he did not object to in the slightest degree. As he ate he noticed half a dozen other patients who were also breakfasting in bed while others were walking about the ward, or sitting in reclining chairs, reading or talking with one another. Some of these had crutches with them, while others wore bandages or limped along with the aid of canes. Bruce, looked all around him in a vain search for some well man, and then innocently asked the nurse how it happened that everybody in the room seemed to be lame or disabled in some way. The nurse smiled at his simplicity and then replied: "They're brought here because they are disabled, for this is a hospital, where broken limbs are set and the sick made well again. You'll have to stay here until you are cured; and if you lie quiet now, in a few days you will be able to walk about like the others you see there."

Then, having advised the young sufferer not to talk or exert himself in any way, she departed with the breakfast tray and Bruce, fatigued by the slight exertion of eating, closed his eyes and was soon sound asleep.

It was after ten o'clock when he awoke suddenly and found the nurse and two or three gentlemen standing at the foot of his bed. One of these gentlemen had a long white beard, gold spectacles, and an exceedingly benevolent air.

"And so this is the brave little fire-lad, is it?" he remarked, with a very kindly smile, as the nurse whispered something in his ear, and in another moment a tall, white screen was placed about the bed, the blanket and sheet drawn up and then Bruce felt shooting pains through his right leg as the head surgeon and his assistants removed the bandages to see how his wounds were getting on. He fully believed that they were cutting his leg off, and after a pain a little sharper than the others he asked, "isn't it most off yet?"

They all smiled at his words and the old gentleman answered in reassuring tones, "no, my son, that leg of yours will be as good as ever in three weeks and you'll live to be a first class fireman yet or I'm very much mistaken."

Then the bandages were quickly replaced, the bed-clothing drawn up, and, when the attendant had removed the screen, Bruce saw the physicians gathered around Skinny the Swiper. The boy set his teeth hard, but uttered no sound, as the bandages were taken from his arm and shoulder and fresh liniment applied to the wounded parts. Bruce could see him watching the faces of the doctors with sharp, eager eyes, very much as a squirrel might regard any object in which it had some special interest; but nevertheless he did not ask a single question or utter the slightest moan, although once his face turned white with pain and the doctor, knowing that the boy was suffering, remarked in his gentle, professional voice, "one moment more, my boy, and it will be all over. There, now, we'll put the bandages on again and the pain will soon go." Then the doctors continued their tour of the ward, and, as soon as they were out of hearing, Skinny turned to Bruce and said, "maybe dat didn't hurt when der bloke pulled dem rags off."

"Look here!" returned the other, "if you don't think I'm the fireman that carried you out of that building, you'd better ask that tall gentleman with the white whiskers; he knew who I was, the minute he saw me and didn't wait to be introduced either."

"Say boss, is dat on de level?" asked the boy as he raised his head slightly from his pillow and fixed his eyes with the same sharp, searching, squirrel look on Bruce's face.

"It is," said the other.

For a few moments, the boy who had grown up in the streets continued to regard the one who had saved his life with a fixed, eager look, but he said nothing. There were undoubtedly things in his mind that he wanted to say, but for the utterance of which his vocabulary was totally inadequate. So he said nothing but "hully gee!" which might have been taken to mean almost anything, but which Skinny the Swiper intended as an expression of gratitude, admiration, and esteem combined with a solemn oath of loyalty, all condensed into two words, neither one of which can be found in Webster's dictionary.

But Bruce had had experience enough with the boys who swarmed about the door of the quarters to know what Skinny meant, and to him the slangy phrase passed for part at least of what the younger lad had wished to express. He said nothing more, but closed his eyes, which were still red and sore, and when he opened them again a few minutes later, the doctors had departed, half a dozen visitors were in the ward, and John Trask was standing beside his bed and calling him by name.

Chapter XX.

NOW it so happened that at the very moment when Bruce was lying on his back in a ward of the New York hospital, a very pretty young girl, whose name might have been on his lips at that painful point of his career, was walking along a shady garden path, with her arms about the waist of a young girl of her own age and equally pretty. One of these young girls, as the least intelligent of my readers may guess, was Laura Van Kuren; the other was her particular friend, Kitty Harriott. As they walked they turned their heads toward one another and seemed engrossed in an eager conversation.

"Hush!" exclaimed Kitty, as she laid a warning hand on her friend's arm. "Harry might be around somewhere, and I wouldn't have him hear us for the world."

"Harry's up stairs finishing his lessons, so you'll have to put up with me until Mr. Reed lets him loose. He got kept in to-day as usual, but I dare say if he knew you were here he'd climb out of the window and come down into the garden as he did last week."

Kitty colored slightly at Laura's words, and then observed with a show of carelessness, "I'm sure it's a matter of perfect indifference to me whether I see him or not. Boys are nuisances anyway, and besides I wouldn't have him hear what we're saying for all the money in the world."

What Laura and Kitty were talking about will probably never be known, at any rate it does not materially concern the readers of this book. They were discussing some affairs of their own, and there are no secrets or mysteries in the world which are invested with the solemn importance that young girls of fourteen or fifteen bestow upon those which they whisper about as they walk through a garden arm and arm, and with heads bent close together. They were so absorbed in their talk that they were startled to hear a familiar voice calling to them from one of the upper windows of the house, and they looked up to see Harry climb over the sill and then descend like a young monkey to the ground, by means of the wisteria vine, to the great terror of Kitty, who had no brothers of her own and who fairly screamed with fright when Harry pretended to miss his hold of the vine, dropped two or three feet and then caught himself cleverly and slid down the rest of the way, with ease and rapidity.

"Mercy!" cried Kitty to Laura who had watched her brother with apparent indifference, "I don't see how you can stand there like that and look at him. Suppose he should fall and break his head, how would you feel then?"

"Pshaw!" exclaimed Laura carelessly, "he only does that to show off because you're here. I knew he'd be out here the minute he caught sight of us. Got your lessons yet, Harry?" she continued, addressing herself to her brother as he joined them.

"Bother the lessons!" was the boy's reply, "I've got something a great deal more interesting, that I might tell you about if I wanted to. It's something that you, particularly, Miss Laura, would be glad to know."

"Well, what is it?" asked his sister indifferently, "is it anything very important?"

"Important enough to be in the newspaper and for me to go right down town to see about it," rejoined her brother.

"Tell me, what it is, Harry, won't you please?" said Kitty, in the pleading way which she knew he could not resist, and in reply Harry produced a copy of the New York *Herald*, which he had been hiding behind his back, carefully folded it, and then, holding it in front of the young girls' faces, permitted them to read a single sentence before he snatched the paper away again. What they read was: "The name of the injured fireman is Bruce Decker. He was removed to the New York hospital, where he now lies in a precarious condition."

Kitty turned toward Laura, whose face was white and whose teeth were tightly clinched. "Isn't it dreadful?" she cried, as she threw her arm about her friend's waist.

"Let me see the rest of it, Harry!" cried Laura, imperiously, trying to take the paper from her brother's hand.

"No, you don't!" cried the boy, resolutely, as he held the *Herald* out of her reach, "not until you find that ball of mine you said you lost yesterday."

"Harry!" called a stern voice near them, and the boy turned sharply round to find his tutor, Mr. Reed, advancing rapidly toward him. "Go back to your room at once, Harry!" said Mr. Reed, sternly; and before the boy could reply his sister tore the paper from his grasp and ran off with it at the top of her speed.

"Come back with that!" cried her brother, as he started in pursuit, but the angry voice of his tutor recalled him before he had gone twenty paces, and he marched into the house very red in the face, and casting angry glances behind him at the two girls, who were now sitting in the summer-house, eagerly reading the long account of the fire at which Bruce had so nearly lost his life. When they had finished it Laura drew a long breath, and then burst into tears.

"Don't cry, dear," said Kitty, as she wiped a tear or two from her own face, "I'm sure he's not badly hurt and will be all right again in a very few days."

"It would be dreadful if he were to die without ever finding out the mystery of his birth," wailed Laura. "Oh, dear, if I only knew where to find him I would write him a letter or go down to see him."

"The paper says he's at the New York hospital," said Kitty. "Why don't you go down there this very day? I think it would be just too romantic and interesting for words."

Laura sprang to her feet and wiped the tears from her eyes with a swift movement of her hand. "I'll do it," she said. "I'll find out where the New York hospital is and how to get there, and I'll start this very minute. Harry thought he was so smart because he read it in the paper first, and was going down there himself all so bold and gay, but he'll find out when he does get there that I've been there before him."

Kitty's face flushed with excitement. She thought it the most romantic thing in the world that Laura should run the risk of displeasing her father by making a long journey all by herself to an unknown part of the town simply to sit by the bedside of a daring young fireman who had been injured while going into a burning building to save a human life. The paper said that he was lying in a "precarious condition," but neither one of the two girls knew what that long word signified, and they did not dare to ask anyone.

"Come up to my room with me, I'm going to get ready now," said Laura, as she led the way into the house.

A quarter of an hour later Harry, who was moodily poring over his Latin grammar and wondering whether Bruce had been severely hurt or not, saw from his seat by the window the two girls crossing the garden and disappearing through a side gate. He wondered idly where they were going to, and then he fell to thinking about how to get even with his sister for the trick she had played him that morning, and he was engaged in this manner when Mr. Reed suddenly entered the room and asked him what progress he was making with his lessons, The boy took up his book again with a sigh that was so deep that the tutor asked him if he was sick or if anything serious had happened.

"No," he replied, "nothing has happened to me, but I'm afraid something awful has happened to Bruce." And then he told the tutor what he had read in the *Herald*, and Mr. Reed becoming very much interested went out and found the paper where the young girls had dropped it in the summer house, and then returned to his pupil's room and said, "I'm afraid he's badly injured and I'm very sorry for it, for he was a very manly, polite young man, and I should judge from the account in the newspaper that he had showed himself to be a brave one as well. I really think you ought to go down to the hospital and see how he is getting along."

Harry leaped to his feet, but Mr. Reed restrained him by saying firmly, "not until your lessons are finished. If you can recite them to me within an hour, we will start at once."

With this incentive to work, Harry returned to his task with such industry and enthusiasm, that when his tutor returned at the close of the hour he found his pupil able to recite his lessons without a single mistake, which was altogether an unusual condition of things with him. Then putting on his hat, Mr. Reed told Harry to accompany him and they started for the elevated railroad together.

Chapter XXI.

"I'LL not shake hands with you, Bruce, but I'd like too, and so would all the men at the quarters," was Mr. Trask's greeting as he seated himself beside the bed of the injured boy. I don't think that arm of yours will stand much shaking for some weeks to come, but we're all proud of you nevertheless." The boy's face flushed with pleasure, and his eyes grew dim for the chief had never spoken to him in such a strain before, and besides he had fancied for a month or two past that his superior rather looked down upon him as a boy who was good for nothing except to bed down horses and make himself generally useful about the quarters. To be sure he did not quite understand why Mr. Trask should say that all the men wanted to shake hands with him, for he had but a hazy remembrance of the events of the previous day, and did not know that his name had been published in the papers with an account of his bravery in saving a boy's life. He did not know what to say, so he simply remarked. " thank you sir."

The chief was silent for a moment and then went on, "well I suppose you've had enough of the fire department by this time, but when you get well I'll see to it that you don't lose anything by what you did yesterday. I had a talk with Mr. Dewsnap, and he'll find a good position somewhere in case you don't want to come back to the quarters again."

Bruce's lips quivered and an expression of dismay came into his face: "What!" he cried piteously, "leave the department the minute I begin to like it! Why, chief, what have I done that you should want to treat me in that way?"

"Then you're not scared of the service by finding yourself laid up in a hospital, are you?" said the chief inquiringly.

"Scared out of it?" echoed the boy, "Why should I be scared out of it? I don't remember everything that happened yesterday but I know that fire was the grandest thing I was ever at in my life. Why, I wouldn't take all the money in the world for my experience yesterday.

I used to hear my father tell about fires, and going into burning buildings and up on the tops of high roofs but I never had any idea of what the service really was until I found myself following the men with that big, cold, clammy hose in my hand. Please Chief Trask, let me stay at the quarters. I'll do anything you want, if you'll only let me go to fires with the men."

"That's right, my boy!" cried the chief heartily. "I like to hear you talk that way. I've been thinking for some time past that you were getting tired of the monotony of the thing and were looking out for a chance to better yourself, and then when you got hurt yesterday, I was afraid it had taken all the ambition out of you, But don't be afraid, you can stay with us as long as you like, and as soon as you're well again, I'll see to it that you go out on the truck along with the rest of the men.

"That's all I ask for, Chief," said Bruce, eagerly, trying to raise his head from the pillow as he spoke, and then letting it fall again from sheer weakness. "The work was getting rather tiresome down there and I hated to be left alone when all the men were away at fires. But if you'll only let me go with them, I won't ask anything more of you."

Then Chief Trask went away promising to come again soon, and Skinny, who had watched him closely through his small squirrel eyes, now turned and said: "Hay boss, dat was de chief of de bat'lion, I've seen him lots of times." And it was evident from the boy's manner that he regarded his friend and preserver with much greater respect than before.

A church clock in the neighborhood had just finished striking eleven, when Miss Ingraham the day nurse, came to Bruce's bedside and said, "There's a young lady down stairs who wishes to see you; do you feel well enough to talk any more?"

A young lady to see him! Bruce wondered, who could it possibly be, and then a look came into his face that made the young lady in the white cap and plaid dress smile, for she guessed from it that it was someone in whom he was deeply interested, so she simply said "I'll send for her to come up," and three minutes later Bruce's heart gave a great bound and then seemed to stand almost still as he saw Laura Van Kuren pause for a moment in the doorway and then walk directly towards his bed.

"Bruce," she said, as she bent down beside him, "are you very much hurt? Oh I was so, so sorry when I read in the paper that you were precarious, and so I came right down to see you."

Of course Bruce had not the slightest idea of what she meant by his being precarious, for he did not know that his exploit had been mentioned in the papers at all, but then Laura often used long words which she found in her favorite books, and he had become accustomed to this peculiarity of hers, and seldom inquired what she meant when the language happened to seem vague and unintelligible.

"No, I'm not badly hurt," he answered cheerfully, " but I say, though, it was splendid of you to come down and see me and I'm ever so much obliged to you. Did you come all alone? Where's Harry?"

I came down here all alone," replied the young girl solemnly, "and you mustn't tell Harry a word about it, because I'd get into awful trouble if you did. Now promise you'll never say a word about it."

Bruce promised readily enough, and then Laura went on : " It would be awful if you had died without finding out the secret of your birth. Only think, you might go to Heaven and never know your own relations when you saw them there and they might be the very nicest people there too."

Bruce could not help laughing at the young girl's serious manner of talking about what she persisted in calling the mystery of his birth. His mind was full of the fire department just

Laura visits Bruce in the hospital.—*Page 196.*

then, and of the bright prospects which Chief Trask had opened to him by promising to allow him to go to all the fires just as if he were a regular member of the company. So he told Laura that at that moment he had no opportunity to pursue the investigations in which she seemed to take so much interest, but he assured her that the moment he found himself well enough to leave the hospital he would continue his search for the tall dark man with the scar across his face whom they both agreed was in some way identified with his early life.

At the end of fifteen minutes Laura went away promising to write him a letter as soon as possible, and leaving him with the cheering assurance that Harry would be down as soon as he had either learned his lessons or escaped from his tutor. Indeed during the whole of her visit she was haunted by an awful fear that her brother had clambered down the wisteria vine and might enter the door at any moment.

Harry did not appear until an hour or more after his sister had gone. Mr. Reed was with him and they had stopped to buy a basket of fruit as a present for the injured boy. Harry was overflowing with sympathy, and Mr. Reed was very much more cordial than he had ever been before.

"I suppose," said the tutor as he and his pupil were taking their leave, "that you have not many friends in town to come to visit."

"Oh, I've had two callers already this morning before you came," replied Bruce. "Chief Trask came first and then—

The boy stopped short, colored, hesitated, and then went on, "and there was another friend of mine who came. She just went away a little while ago."

Both his visitors noticed his hesitation and Harry wondered if it could be possible that his sister had been down there ahead of him, but he said nothing to Mr. Reed of his suspicions. He resolved however to get at the truth of the matter so that he might have something fresh to taunt his sister with the next time they quarrelled.

It is doubtful if the whole city of New York contained a happier boy than the one who was lying, sorely wounded and with his eyes inflamed and almost blinded, in a narrow white cot in a common hospital ward. The sun was shining brightly through the tall windows, and the distant hum and roar of the great city sounded faintly in his ears. He knew that it would be many weeks, perhaps months, before he could hope to resume the career which had been interrupted so suddenly the day before, and to a boy who had never known a day's illness in his life the prospect of a long, irksome confinement was anything but pleasant. Nevertheless, Bruce Decker felt that he had a great deal to make him happy just then.

First of all he realized that he had done his duty in facing danger the first time that he was called upon, and Chief Trask's encouraging words had sounded more agreeably in his ears than anything that he had ever heard before. Moreover, the fact that not only the chief but Harry and Laura Van Knren had come at once to his bedside was another reason for his contented state of mind. But beside all this the memory of the exciting events of the day before filled his mind. There had come over him while he stood with a hose in his hand amid the smoke and blaze of the burning building an overwhelming sense of the importance and dignity of his calling, and it had seemed to him at that moment that he was no longer a mere boy, tolerated at the quarters because he could run errands and take care of horses, but a fireman in the truest sense of the word—one whose duty it was to go without fear wherever his chief led him, and to be ready, if necessary, to sacrifice his life (as his father had done before him) to save another's. And now as he rested quietly in his bed the soldierly feeling had full possession of his soul. If he had ever cherished any serious thought of leaving the department and seeking employment in some other walk of life, that feeling was now entirely submerged by one of loyal devotion to the department which he had served, and to which he would return as soon as he could leave his bed, with a steadfast purpose far deeper than the enthusiasm which had influenced him before.

Taking all these things into consideration, it is not to be wondered at that a right-minded, brave young lad like Bruce Decker should have been positively happy in spite of his hurts as he lay there, one of twenty-four patients in the casualty ward. But although he did not know it, he had another reason for thankfulness, for he had attached to himself a new friend—a friend who was bound to prove of infinite service to him in untangling some of the threads which had caused him so much anxious thought of late. That new friend was lying in the cot next to him, silently watching him through a pair of sharp blue eyes.

Skinny the Swiper was a child of the New York streets, one of those boys who could not remember having had any home or kindred, and who, from his earliest recollection, had been living as best he could by selling papers, blacking boots, or doing anything that he could turn his hand to. His wits, naturally sharp, had been developed to a remarkable degree of precocity by his rough contact with the world until they had made him more than a match for any of the lads with whom he consorted. He had known very little kindness in his dozen years of life, and possibly it was for that reason that his heart went out in gratitude to the boy who had saved him, but Skinny was a lad of few words, and although he looked searchingly at the other and probably thought a great deal, it was not until late in the afternoon that he ventured to speak of what was uppermost in his thoughts. Then he raised himself slightly on his elbow and said: "Hay, boss, I seen dat young lady before, onct."

Bruce did not like the idea of discussing such a superior being as Laura Van Kuren with a grimy little boy of the streets, and besides he did not believe that Skinny had ever seen her, so he answered rather curtly, "No, I guess you're mistaken; that young lady doesn't live in the same street with you."

"Who said she did?" demanded the boy. "But I seen her all de same. Besides I don't live in no street at all."

"Well, where did you see her then?"

"I seen her way up near de Harlem. Her folks has got a big house dere, an' one day when I was walkin' by I stopped ter look troo de railin' and she come up and gimme some grapes. She's a jim dandy, dat young lady is."

"But how came you away up there?" inquired Bruce, in some amazement.

"I went up dere fer a man wot useter git me to run errands onct in a while, and dat's de way I seen her," replied Skinny.

"What sort of errands did you have to do up there? I should think that would be pretty far out of your beat," continued Bruce, with an idle curiosity to learn something of his new friend.

"Oh! I went up dere lots o' times on most partick'ler business," responded Skinny. "Dere was a bloke useter send me ter carry letters to a big house dat had evergreens in front of it and a porch over de door. Deres was an' old gent lived dere, but now he's gone ter Yurrup or Africky or some place or nudder."

And now it was Bruce's turn to be interested. "Was there a side door to the house, with vines hanging over it?" he asked.

"Cert," replied Skinny, "an' an old gent dat giv me a quarter two or tree times. An' twict he sent me in de kitchen an' de lady wot cooked dere gimme a steak an' pertaters an' coffee. Dey never watched me needer, an' I mighter swiped some spoons on'y dey used me so white."

Bruce's head, which had been lifted slightly from the pillow during this conversation, now fell back from sheer weariness, and for a few moments the boy remained absolutely quiet, wondering if it could be possible that he had found in this street Arab someone who could enlighten him in regard to the mystery which had puzzled him so much and awakened such a deep interest in the heart of Laura Van Kuren.

"Who was the man who used to send you up there on errands?" inquired Bruce, after a brief silence.

"I never knowed his name. He was a bloke dat useter hang out at a place in Eldridge street, and he seen me around dere an' gimme a job now an' den. We useter call him Scar-Faced Charley."

"Well, what sort of a looking man was he?" persisted Bruce, trying not to betray the deep interest that he felt.

"He was a tall feller, an' had a black beard an' a scar acrost his face," said Skinny.

Bruce asked no more questions, and the young newsboy soon after fell into a doze, leaving the other free to pursue his thought. It seemed to him now that he had at last found a clue to the identity of the man who had known his father, and whom he never doubted for a moment was the same one who had sent Skinny on errands to Mr. Dexter's house. The more he thought of it the more excited he became, and in his weak condition the excitement soon made itself manifest in his face, so that Miss Ingraham, pausing for a moment beside his cot, noticed the condition of her patient, felt of his pulse, and then called the doctor to see if any change for the worse had taken place. The boy seemed to be on the verge of a fever, so the doctor gave him a quieting draught and bade him compose his mind, if possible, and go to sleep.

The next day Bruce awoke feeling calmer and refreshed. The fever of the day before had left him, and when Miss Ingraham made her morning rounds she found him looking so much better that she smiled encouragingly upon him, and told him that he was on the high road to recovery.

"Is there anything you would like me to do for you?" said the nurse, kindly.

"Yes," replied the boy timidly, "if it is not too much trouble for you, I would like to have you write me a letter. I can't use my hands yet and there's a friend of mine to whom I wish to write."

The nurse, who was accustomed to requests of this sort, brought pen and paper to his bedside, sat down and said: "Well, what shall I write?"

"You may begin with Dear Miss Laura," said Bruce and Miss Ingraham smiled to herself as she wrote it. The letter, which was concocted between them, read as follows:

"DEAR MISS LAURA:
Something happened just after you went away yesterday that I thought would interest you. In the bed next to mine is a small boy whom I pulled out of the building that was on fire. As soon as you had gone he told me that he had seen you before, but I did not believe him. I asked him where and he said up near the Harlem river where you live. Then I asked him how he came to be up there, and he said that a man used to send him on errands to a house which I am sure from his description is Mr. Dexter's. I asked him who the man was but he did not

know. All he could tell me was that he was a tall, dark man with a black beard and a scar across his face. What do you think of that? It looks to me as if I could run him down with the help of Skinny, the boy who told me that, and as soon as I get well again I will start after him.

Thanking you for your great kindness in coming to see me, I am,

Yours very respectfully,
Bruce Decker."

Then, having cautioned Miss Ingraham not to reveal to anybody the contents of his letter, he begged her to stamp and mail it to the address which he gave her, and this she readily promised to do.

Chapter XXII.

MR. VAN KUREN was seated at the breakfast table when the morning mail arrived and the servant placed the letters and papers in his hand. Glancing hurriedly at them, he noticed that one envelope bore the inscription of the New York hospital and was addressed to Miss Laura Van Kuren. The children had told him about Bruce's misfortune and he guessed at once that the letter was from him. A cloud came across his face at once for he rightly considered his daughter too young to write to and receive letters from young boys, especially those of whom he knew as little as he did of Bruce. He said nothing at the time but slipped the letter into his pocket and as soon as breakfast was over bade Laura follow him into the library.

"Here is a letter for you, my daughter," he said quietly, "and you may read it now."

The young girl colored up to the roots of her hair as she opened the letter and hastily read it. Then she handed it to her father to read and she knew from the expression of his face that its contents were anything but pleasing to him. When he had finished it he said to her sternly: "I am surprised indeed, Laura, that you should discuss family secrets which you do not yourself comprehend, with a boy who is a complete stranger to us all, and I am grieved to learn that you went down to the hospital to visit him without saying anything about it to me or to your aunt. How did you ever come to mention the name of Mr. Dexter to this boy and how did he ever learn anything about this dark bearded man with the scar? Years ago, as you and Harry know perfectly well, you were both forbidden to go near the Dexter house or ask any questions concerning him or his family. I had excellent reasons for not discussing with you matters which you are still too young to understand. Now tell me how you came to seek information from this young rascal with whom you are carrying on a secret correspondence."

Laura, who had listened to her father's words with downcast eyes, bit her lips angrily when she heard Bruce called "a young rascal." She did not wish to tell her father the secret which she felt belonged by right not to her but to Bruce, and yet she knew that she must make some sort of reply, so she answered after a

Then Laura began to cry.—*Page 203*.

moment's hesitation : "He knew Mr. Dexter because he was sent up there on an errand that day that he found Harry with his sprained ankle and brought him home. So we got to talking about him and I told him that Harry and I had been forbidden to go near the house."

Then Laura began to cry and her father, having peremptorily ordered her not to reply to Bruce's letter, started for his office, stopping a moment to tell Mr. Reed what had happened, and to bid him put a stop at once to the intimacy with the young fireman who had, as he imagined, transgressed the law of hospitality by writing letters to the young girl.

It was a dreary day for the brother and sister when they learned from the lips of the tutor that their father had forbidden them to have anything further to do with their new friend whom they both liked so much. Harry was particularly displeased because he declared that it was all Laura's fault for sneaking off by herself to visit him and then getting him to write letters to her, which she should have known was altogether improper. Laura on her part declared that if Harry had not been so hateful she would never have thought of doing anything to spite him and ended the discussion by declaring angrily, that she thought boys a nuisance and she was never going to have anything more to do with any of them so long as she lived. That afternoon Kitty Harriott came to see her, and on learning the dreadful news, proceeded to console her as well as she could, assuring her friend that it would all come out right after all just as it did in the story books of which they were so fond.

During the first few days of his confinement in the hospital, Bruce found that the time hung very heavy on his hands, that his wounds were painful, his spirits low, and if it had not been for the occasional visits of his friends from the quarters, it is possible that he would have come to the conclusion that after all a fireman's life was not a happy one. He was rather surprised that the Van Kuren children neither came to see him again nor wrote to him, but the truth was that Harry and Laura who were, in spite of their many faults, tactful children and thoughtful of the feelings of others, had decided that it would be best to keep their friend in ignorance of their father's commands. "Because," they argued, "he has a hard enough time of it now, lying there all day in the hospital, and if he learns that our father has put a stop to our friendship with him, it may make him worse, and it will certainly not make him any happier than he is."

Bruce, of course, knew nothing about this, but imagined that the children would come to see him or write him again at the first opportunity. As he grew better he found himself taking an interest in the events of the ward in which he lay, and it was not long before he had made the acquaintance of a few of the patients who were well enough to walk about and gossip with the occupants of the different beds. Most of the people in the casualty ward were working men who had met with accidents, and he noticed to his surprise that some of them seemed in no hurry to get well, and always limped in the most grievous fashion when any of the doctors were about.

It was Skinny the Swiper who explained this phenomenon to him by remarking that these invalids lived better in the hospital than they did at home and at much less expense, and were therefore perfectly willing to stay there all winter and board at the expense of the city without doing any hard work.

There were other men, however, who took their confinement much to heart and had no anxiety save to get out again and go to work for their wives and families. Bruce noticed, also, that the most intelligent men about him always yielded to the wishes of the physicians, took the medicines that were given them, and reposed faith in the wisdom of the medical practitioners, while the more ignorant ones did not hesitate to affirm that the doctors did not know their business, and that they themselves were capable of determining what medicine they should take and how their wounds should be treated. Having very little to do but lie on his back, and notice what went on about him, the boy acquired no small knowledge of human life and nature by his observations in the hospital ward.

As to Skinny the Swiper, he proved an uncomplaining patient and, although rather taciturn from force of habit, was at times very entertaining in his accounts of life in what he called "de Fort' ward" where he lived, and his comments on the people about him.

It was Skinny who awakened a burst of laughter one morning by suddenly calling out to one of the patients who had no desire to leave the hospital and return to his work, "Cheese it, Welch, you're limpin' on de wrong leg this morning! De doctor 'll drop to yer." And it was Skinny who learned to imitate the voices of the other men and would often break the silence of the early night with his monkey-like drollery. He regarded Bruce as his preserver, and although he said but little in token of his gratitude, the other soon began to feel that he could rely upon the tough little news boy to render him any service that he might ask of him. And as day succeeded day, he carefully studied the character of his new friend, in order to determine whether it would be safe to trust him with the secret which as yet he had shared with no one but Laura. Then he remembered his promise to the young girl and determined that no matter what might happen he would say nothing without first obtaining her permission.

At last the day came when the house surgeon, pausing in front of the boys' beds, remarked: "Well, you two young men seem to be doing quite nicely, so I think you can get ready to leave here at the end of the week." By this time both boys had progressed so far that they were able to walk about the ward and eat their meals in the dining room instead of having them brought to their bed-side. They were not strong by any means, but it was no longer necessary for them to remain in the hospital and their beds were needed for other patients. Bruce was delighted at the prospect of going and instantly wrote to Chief Trask to tell him the news. But Skinny heard the doctor's words with passive indifference and did not seem to care much whether he went or stayed.

"Where are you going to when you leave here?" said Bruce to his companion as he folded up his letter and addressed the envelope.

"Dunno" was the laconic reply.

Bruce paused in his work and looked at the other with surprise. "Do you mean to tell me that you haven't any place to go to after you leave here?" he demanded.

"No place in partick'lar" answered Skinny. "Mebbe I'll go down to der Newsboy's Home an' brace de boss for a week's lodgins, an' a couple of dimes fer ter buy extrys wid."

The boy announced his intentions in a matter-of-fact way that showed plainly what his manner of life had been, but Bruce was amazed to think that anyone could leave a sick bed and go out without friends to face the world as coolly and calmly as if he were going to a comfortable home. All this time the boys had been sitting in extension chairs beside their beds and when Bruce had sealed his letter he went out to the closet in which his clothes and a few things that Chief Trask had sent him were kept, took from an inside vest pocket his pocket-book and found that it contained just eight dollars and forty-four cents. Taking exactly half of his fortune, he went back to where Skinny was seated and placed it in his lap.

"There," he remarked, "that's just half my pile, Skinny, and perhaps the time will come when I shall want you to divide your pile with me."

Skinny looked at the money in his lap and then picked it up, carefully counted it, and rung one of the silver dollars with his teeth as if in doubt of its being genuine. Then he fixed his keen little blue eyes on Bruce and seemed to be trying to find some ulterior motive for his generosity. It was seldom, indeed, that anyone had reposed confidence in Skinny to the extent of lending him nearly five dollars, and he could not understand why anyone should do such a thing unless he had some object to gain. But his scrutiny of the boy's clear, honest face failed to reveal to him any secret or sinister design, and so, after a moment's hesitation, he said cautiously "Is dis on de level?"

"That's all right," remarked Bruce, who had winced perceptibly under the boy's squirrel like gaze, "You're welcome to that as long as you choose to keep it."

"Say, boss," continued Skinny after another pause, during which he carefully thumbed over his suddenly acquired wealth, "dat's de white ting ter do, and I'll hump meself when I gets well to pay it off."

Bruce had winced under the boy's sharp look because he felt that he suspected him of some ulterior motive, and he knew that he had an ulterior motive, which was to place Skinny under still further obligations to him in order that he might be depended upon to aid him in his search for the man who had once known his father. Never since the morning when the newsboy recognized Laura Van Kuren had Bruce referred in any way to the mysterious scarred and bearded stranger by whom the boy had been employed. He did not wish to exhibit any interest in him. The time would come for that, he said to himself, when he had left the hospital, and it was with this object in view that he had devoted a great deal of his time during his convalescence to cultivating an intimacy with Skinny and deepening in the heart of that young vagabond the feelings of gratitude and regard which he already felt for the gallant young fire laddie who had carried him from the burning building.

It was Saturday morning when the boys said good bye to Miss Ingraham and their fellow patients in the casualty ward, and went out once more into the open street. Together they trudged along Fifteenth Street to Broadway where Bruce took a car for the quarters, not feeling strong enough to walk any further, and Skinny kept on toward Third Avenue, intending to go down to the Newsboys' Home. Just before they parted, Skinny surprised his friend by saying in a careless way, "Boss, you reck'lect that party I was speakin' of as sent me on de errands? Well, I kin fin' him any time yer want him. Dat's all." Then he nodded his head and slouched across the street, a grotesque, ragged figure, while Bruce climbed into the horse-car and wondered how on earth the boy could ever have discovered that he felt any interest whatever in the man of whom they had spoken but once. But Bruce did not know how contact with the rough side of city life sharpens the senses of the young, nor did he know that, during those long days in the hospital ward, he had been very closely watched and studied by the little vagabond beside him.

Chapter XXIII.

MEANTIME things had not been going on smoothly at the home of the Van Kuren children. Mr. Van Kuren, although a devoted and careful father, was so much engrossed in his business that he had comparatively little time to devote to his children, and since the death of their mother, their education had necessarily been left largely in the hands of tutors, governesses and instructors of all sorts. The discovery that the young boy from the fire department whom he had been inclined to regard with so much favor had taken advantage of his intimacy with the children to conduct a clandestine correspondence with the daughter of the house, annoyed Mr. Van Kuren excessively, and he determined to take immediate steps to prevent any repetition of the offense or continuance of the friendship. It was chiefly for this purpose that he finally made up his mind to do what he had long contemplated, and one morning he summoned both children to his study, and threw them into a fever of excitement and delight by bidding them prepare at once for a trip to Europe.

"But must we start to-morrow?" demanded Laura. "Why, I never can get ready in the world."

"Very well," replied her father with a smile. "If you're not ready, you may remain at home while Harry, your aunt, Mr. Reed and I will take the trip. Shall I send word to the steamship office that we only need tickets for four?"

"No, no, no," cried Laura, jumping up and down excitedly, "don't do that. I'll go right away now and get ready. I'd die if I had to stay home while you and Harry went off."

Then both children set about the work of packing up their things and of writing one or two good-bye letters to the friends whom they where leaving behind.

"Did papa say how long we were to remain away?" asked Laura as she paused in the middle of a letter,

"No," answered her brother carelessly, "but probably quite a while. I don't care how long we stay. It will be lots of fun over there, and ever so much better than learning stupid lessons and staying in one place all the time. I guess I'll write a letter to Bruce and tell him that we're going to Europe to-morrow. I won't say anything about papa getting hold of that letter, and when we come back maybe we'll be allowed to ask him up here again."

So Bruce learned the next day, at the very moment when the steamer was leaving her dock, that his friends had sailed away across the ocean and did not know when they would see him again. Europe seemed so far away to the young boy, and a trip across the ocean such a formidable undertaking, that it seemed to him that he had said good-bye to them forever, and that if they did come back at all, they would never be the same.

Now Mr. Van Kuren had purposely said nothing to his children about the probable length of their stay, but he had really determined to remain with them abroad for at least a year, with the intention of carrying on their education, at the same time giving them the advantages of travel in foreign lands. Once across the ocean, he was satisfied that his daughter would forget the young fireman for whom he feared she cherished a childish liking, and so, as soon as the steamer had passed Sandy Hook, he dismissed Bruce altogether from his mind, and busied himself with thoughts of the days that lay before him.

Harry's letter to his young friend proved a genuine shock, and for fully twenty-four hours after receiving it, Bruce walked about the quarters, or sat in his accustomed seat in the corner, in a condition of dejection that did not escape the notice of Tom Brophy or the chief, for they both spoke of it, and both of them hoped that after distinguishing himself as he had, the boy would not allow himself to fall back into the state of discontent and indifference that had previously annoyed them.

At the end of twenty-four hours, however, the boy suddenly regained his good spirits. During his period of gloom he had argued with and succeeded in convincing himself that, after all, the departure of his two cherished friends for Europe was the very best thing that could have happened to him. "It made me sore," he acknowledged to himself, "to go up there to their big house and see all the nice things they had, and then come back to my work again. If a fellow has got to work for his living as I have, he'd much better keep away from rich folks, and not have any friends who can spend a dollar where he can spend a cent. Everybody says I've made a good beginning, and now I am going to keep right on. If I have any spare time, I'll spend it with that Skinny, working up what Laura calls the mystery of my birth."

He smiled as he thought of the deep interest with which she used to discuss his affairs, and then a shade of sadness crossed his face as he remembered that she was at that moment out on the ocean, and that he might never see her again. Then his good sense acted as a tonic to his resolution, and he went about his duties determined that when she did return, she would find him changed and improved almost beyond recognition.

His confinement in the hospital had left him in no condition to do a full day's work, and so at the chief's suggestion he spent a good part of his time out-of-doors, either walking about the streets near the quarters, or else riding up to Central Park, and strolling about in its pleasant paths, where he could enjoy the bright sunshine and the clear, fresh air to his heart's content.

It was during one of these rambles that he determined to devote some of his leisure time, and he had a great deal of it now owing to his state of health, to seek out his new boy friend and asking him to aid him in his work of investigation. Bruce was by nature a deliberate, slow-thinking boy, who seldom acted on the impulse of the moment, and had a habit of devoting a great deal of thought to whatever he went about. He was naturally secretive, too, and up to this time, he had made a confidant of nobody except Laura Van Kuren; not even to Chief Trask or Tom Brophy had he spoken a single word in regard to the important matter which had taken up such a large share of his thoughts.

Having once made up his mind that Skinny was a boy to be depended on, he did not start off at the very instant of his decision to seek him out, but with characteristic reserve waited until the next morning, and then, having obtained a leave of absence until the afternoon, started for the lower part of the city. In front of a tall brick building, not far from what was once Chatham Street, but is now Park Row, he paused and looked up. It was the Newsboys' Lodging House, and the gentleman who stood in the doorway and asked him what he wanted, was the superintendent.

Bruce made known his errand, and the superintendent shook his head doubtfully. "I don't know where you'll find that boy Skinny," he replied "he turned up here some time ago with a story about having been in the hospital, and I must say he looked as if he'd been through some trouble or other, put up here for a while and then disappeared, and I haven't seen him since."

"Well, he told the truth about being in the hospital," rejoined the visitor stoutly, "for I was there with him, and now I'd like to find him for a very particular reason."

"I guess," replied the superintendent, "there are a good many people would like to find him for some particular reason, but I don't know where he is, unless he's selling papers around City Hall Square. I'll ask the other boys to-night if they know anything about him, and then if you can drop around to-morrow, I may be able to tell you something."

Bruce turned away dejected and distrustful. He was afraid that Skinny would drift out of his ken. "I was foolish to let him have that money," he said to himself, "because he'll never show up again for fear of being asked for it."

Chapter XXIV.

AND now let us return to the newsboy, and trace his footsteps from the time he left his benefactor on the corner of Broadway. He stood on the street corner watching with his small, sharp eyes the street car until it was out of sight, then he turned and trudged on to Third Avenue, where he swung himself on board another car and was carried down to the lower part of the city. He went direct to the lodging-house, and, as the superintendent had said, told what was regarded at the time as an invention of his own, about his mishap at the fire, and his experience in the hospital, and was finally allowed to become a lodger for a short time on credit. He said nothing about the four dollars and twenty-two cents that Bruce had loaned him, and which he still had in his pocket. He had already determined to devote that sum to a special purpose, and to depend upon what he could pick up by selling newspapers or running errands to defray his expenses. He had often slept and eaten in the lodging house before, and, when the boys came trooping in just before supper time, there were many among them who knew him and came over to ask him where he had been. The general opinion among the boys, and it was shared by the superintendent also, was that Skinny had been sent to Blackwell's Island for some misdemeanor, and had simply invented the hospital and fire story to shield his good name.

"Dat's what happens to me fer goin' ter work reg'lar," said the boy to himself. "Before I was in dat factory a day it took fire, an' I hadn't even had de time to learn de way out."

That night the boy sat down to supper with a hundred or more lads representing a dozen races and nationalities and innumerable callings, though the bulk of them made their living by selling newspapers and blacking boots. Supper over, they repaired to a big schoolroom on the floor above, and there, with slates and pencils and spelling books, endeavored to master the rudiments of an education. Skinny sat down at his desk with the others, and for an hour worked diligently. But every once in a while the remembrance of his friend, the fireman, would come into his mind. He knew intuitively that Bruce was interested in the young girl who had come to see him, and the tall, dark man who must be, the boy reasoned, connected with her in some way. He would make it his business to seek out this man, and all that he could learn about him he would place at the service of his new friend.

Born and brought up in the slums, having learned his trade in the streets and in the face of the sharp, juvenile competition which goes on there, Skinny was well suited to prosecute a search of the kind that now engrossed his attention. The next morning he was up at daybreak with the rest of the boys, and after breakfast betook himself to the big newspaper buildings where the presses were turning out the damp, freshly printed sheets by the thousands. Withdrawing from his hoarded capital half a dollar, Skinny invested it in a stock of morning papers, and then stationed himself near the entrance to the Bridge. By nine o'clock his stock was exhausted, and he had also secured about twenty papers which he had begged from passers by who had read and were about to discard them. These he had also disposed of, and he was now more than half a dollar richer than he had been the night before. Satisfied with his morning's work, he returned to the lodging house and rested there until it was time to resume business with the afternoon papers as his stock in trade. The various editions of these kept him busy during the afternoon, and netted him half a dollar. Then he went home, exhausted with his hard work, ate his supper, spent an hour in the schoolroom, and then went to bed.

For several weeks he labored industriously, and then beginning to tire of newspaper selling, he determined to find some other job.

Early one morning he bent his steps in the direction of Chatham Square, whence he walked along the Bowery till he came to Grand Street, and then, turning to the east, walked on until he found himself in the Jewish quarter of the town. As he walked he cast furtive and suspicious glances about him from time to time, for the exigencies of his life had taught him to be sharp and cunning, and distrustful of other people. It was seven o'clock by this time, and the street was full of girls hurrying toward the factories in which they worked. Turning into a side street the boy slunk along the pavement, and finally stopped and fixed his eyes on an old ramshackle building, the upper stories of which were occupied as a tenement house, while the ground floor was used as a sort of office. For some time the boy stood looking intently at this building from the opposite side of the street, and then seeing no sign of life in the office on the ground floor, he walked away, made a circuit of the neighborhood, and at the end of an hour returned once more; this time he found the office open and within it a small, dried up old man, who was writing in a big leather bound book. To him the boy addressed himself:

"Want any errands run to-day, boss?" he inquired.

"No!" replied the old man, shortly.

"Hey, boss," went on Skinny, "I used ter do odd jobs for dat bloke wid de black whiskers dat wuz here before, and I always done right by him." The old book-keeper fixed his spectacles on his nose, and looked sharply down at the lad who stood before him with upturned face and with his hat on the back of his head.

"Are you the boy that he used to send up town last winter?" demanded the clerk, suspiciously,

"Yes, I used ter take letters fer him way up above de bridge," replied the other.

"Where have you been keeping yourself of late? If you'd been here a few days ago you might have earned a dollar or so, but you boys are never around when you are wanted," continued the book-keeper, speaking in sharp, stern tones.

"Well, ain't dere no chance for me now, boss? I wuz burned out of a factory, carried down de ladder by a mug dat found me burnin' up, and den dey took me to de hospital, and here I am. But where's his nibs gone ter?"

"Yes," said the book-keeper, scornfully, "you've been to the hospital, no doubt, but I guess it was a judge sent you there. But you come in here at twelve o'clock, and perhaps there'll be a little work for you."

"Dat's it all de time," said Skinny to himself, as he walked away. "Wot's de use of doin' de right ting when nobody won't believe yer, and tinks all de time yer been up to der Island? Dat's wot comes of goin' to work reg'lar," he added, and he shook his head with a determination never to do any business in the future except on his own account.

Twelve o'clock found him standing once more in the little office on the side street, and when he entered, the old bookkeeper, who was still making entries in the big leather-bound volume as if he had been at it without a second's interruption all the morning, scarcely raised his eyes, while he said to him: "Do you remember going up to a house above the Harlem river, one day, to take a letter to an old gentleman who lived there?"

"So you've been in the hospital, have you?"—*Page 225*.

"A big, square house, wid evergreens around it?" Yes, I could find it again in de dark."

"Very well," continued the bookkeeper, whose pen did not cease scratching for a single moment, "you'd better go up now and find it, for there's a gentleman up there who may give you a job; but let me give you a bit of advice, young man. Don't remember too much or see too much when you're sent on errands. It's the boys who forget what they see, and the places that they're sent to, who make the most money nowadays. Here's twenty-five cents for car fare, and now you go up there, and you'll find the gentleman whom you politely refer to as 'the bloke with the black whiskers' waiting for you."

Skinny made haste to obey, and within an hour was entering the dark, shady grounds of Mr. Dexter's house with the same furtive, cautious way of looking about him that he had shown further down town. His old acquaintance, the man with the black beard and the deeply-scarred face, was walking up and down the roadway in front of the house, smoking a cigar.

"So you've been in the hospital, have you?" was his salutation. "What sort of a hospital was it? One with bars to the window?"

"Naw, der wan't no bars to de windows. I wuz in de New York hospital, and I'll leave it to de nurse, a dinky lady wot sat up all night wid us, and wore a white cap. Dat's on de level, boss."

The tall man regarded him suspiciously for a moment, and the boy squinted up at him with a defiant look in his sharp eyes that caused the other to smile and say to him in more conciliatory tones: "Well, I've got one or two errands for you to do, and if you do them properly, you'll be well paid for them. If not, you'll come to grief. How would you like to take a little trip into the country, to be gone two or three days? I hope that you have no pressing business engagements in the city that will interfere with the project."

Skinny replied with perfect gravity that he had intended to take dinner with Mr. Vanderbilt that night, but that he would try and get him to excuse him, in which case he observed in his picturesque slang that it would be necessary for him to eat elsewhere, and at an early moment. The tall man was laughing broadly now—he always found a great deal of amusement in Skinny—and so he bade him go into the kitchen and tell the cook to let him have something to eat. "When you are through, come into the library, I want to talk to you."

Chapter XXV.

THE boy partook of a hearty meal in the kitchen of the great house, and while he was eating it, entertained the cook and the other servants with his droll comments on the food that was set before him. Having finished, he washed his face and hands at the sink, bowed politely to those who were in the room, and went up to the library where the master of the house was awaiting him.

"Do you think" said the tall man, "that you could find your way to a place two or three hundred miles from here, do an errand for me without telling everything you know, and then come back?"

"I kin," was Skinny's answer.

"Very well," rejoined the other producing a paper on which was written a number of names " Can you read writing?

Yes, thanks to the night school in the lodging house, Skinny could read, and he said so in accents of just pride mingled with contempt for those who were his inferiors in that point of education.

"All right then," continued the other. "Take this paper and listen to what I tell you. Go up to the village of Rocky Point and try to get work there with some farmer or shopkeeper. That's just for a blind, you know, so that nobody will guess that you've come up there all the way from New York. Perhaps it would be better for you to stop off the train at some other village and walk in on foot. As soon as you get a chance, take a walk out to the cemetery and look around for a grave marked Decker. I think it's the grave of Mary Decker. When you find it, copy the inscription, every word of it, mind, dates and all, and stick it away somewhere where nobody will find it. Then see if there are any other graves in the same plot with the same name. See if there is the grave of a young boy, the son of this Mary Decker there, and if there is a grave without any headstone over it, find out who lies buried there. If there is no other grave, find out from some of the village folks whether this Mary Decker left any children, and if so what has become of them. It may take you a week, or it may take you only a day to do all this, but as soon as you get the information, come back to me and let me know about it. Here is money enough for your fare and other expenses, and perhaps you had better write me a letter as soon as you get settled there. Here is my address, Robert J. Korwein, — Eldridge Street."

Skinny had listened with close attention to all that had been said to him and now, taking the paper with the different names marked on it, he carefully went over it, making a few scratches of his own from time to time which should serve him as memoranda. Then without a word, he took the roll of bills which lay on the table before him, counted them carefully and hid them away in the inner pocket of his ragged jacket.

"I understand, boss," he simply said, "wot time does de train start?"

"To-night at eight" was the reply, "here's a time table and remember to change cars at Syracuse for Oswego. There you will take another train for Rocky Point. Be careful not to attract any attention or set those village fools to gossiping and cackling. Above all, don't let anybody find out that I sent you, or that there's anybody alive who takes any interest in the grave of Mary Decker or in the whereabouts of her son. If you get through this trip all right and find out what I want to know, I'll give you more money than you ever had before in your life."

"Dere won't be no slip-up, nor funny business wid me, boss," said Skinny as he buttoned his coat over the roll of greenbacks. I'll git you dere names and all and I'll probably write yer in two or tree days."

Mr. Korwein accompanied the boy to the gate and, having repeated his caution to observe secrecy and dispatch in his mission, bade him good-bye, and watched him as he walked down the road and finally disappeared from view; then he returned to the front porch of the house, seated himself on the steps, and for some time sat there smoking and thinking. After awhile, he threw away his cigar, pulled a letter from his pocket and read it carefully through. It was dated Paris, and read as follows:

"MY DEAR NEPHEW:

It is a great pleasure to me to hear from you as frequently as I do, and I sincerely hope that you are living up to all that you promised me at our last meeting. I think on the whole, that it is a fortunate thing for me, that you are living in the old homestead, and I am glad that you find the house comfortable. As the years roll by, each one leaves its weight on my shoulders and as I draw nearer to the end I find myself thinking more of the few of my blood who remain. As I told you long ago I have never made a will, fearing that it would bring about an unseemly contest after I had gone. As next of kin you will be my principal heir, and I charge you once more to carefully carry out all the wishes which I have made known to you concerning the small bequests to my faithful servants and others whom I wish to reward.

I have not yet determined when to return to my own country, but it is not improbable that you will see me before the end of the year. Meantime see that the house and grounds are suitably maintained, and write me from time to time concerning your welfare.

Hoping this will find you in good health, I remain,
Your affectionate kinsman,
SAMUEL DEXTER."

When Mr. Korwein had finished reading this letter he replaced it carefully in his pocket, lit another cigar, and resumed his meditations, and if anyone could have looked into his heart at that moment he would have been heard to say to himself something like the following:

"I think that after all I have played my cards wonderfully well and unless some brat turns up with a claim on it nothing can prevent me from inheriting the bulk of the estate. So far he knows nothing about the shop down town, but if he ever finds out about it I shall be ruined. I'll take care that he doesn't though, and, after all, the city is so big, and there are so many people in it, that the chances of his or anybody else's connecting me with that shop are very small indeed. The boy has got some stuff in him and under my tuition he'll amount to something. I think I'll take hold of him if he does this business in the country all right, and give him a steady job, looking after my affairs. He's a smart little brute and knows enough to keep his mouth shut. It's easy enough to get some lawyer to go up there and find out what I want to know but a lawyer would be too smart to suit me; he'd suspect something at once, whereas this kid will think of nothing except the money he's going to get, besides if he did want to blab he'd find no one but some youngster of his own age and class to talk to. I guess I did the best thing I could in sending him up there, but all the same I shall be anxious until he gets back."

At this point in his reflections, the tall, dark bearded man rose to his feet, walked swiftly down the winding path, passed through the front gate, and then went on down below it till he reached the station of the east side of the Elevated railroad. Three quarters of an hour later he entered the little office on Eldridge Street where the book-keeper was still diligently at work on his big ledger.

"How is business to-day?" he asked of his assistant.

"Pretty fair" replied the other, as he handed his chief a batch of letters that had arrived in the morning's mail, and which he had opened and perused. Mr. Korwein took the letters in his hand, pushed open a small swinging door behind the book-keeper's desk and disappeared into the room beyond, leaving the old book-keeper toiling away with his scratching pen as if he had been at it all his life and never expected to stop.

When Skinny the Swiper parted from his employer he walked rapidly down the road which led to the Elevated station, took the train and proceeded to Forty-second Street, and then to the Grand Central Depot. Here he purchased a ticket for Rocky Point, and, finding that he still had an hour to wait, determined to employ his time to good advantage in eating another dinner. The fact that he had partaken of a hasty repast in Mr. Korwein's kitchen two hours before, made no difference to him. Hearty repasts did not come in Skinny's way every day, and he believed in availing himself of every opportunity of the sort that presented itself. He was capable of eating three or four dinners in one day, and nothing at all for two days after, and as he was going into the interior of the country, to a point more distant from the city than any that he had ever previously visited, he determined to fortify himself for the journey with a good, square New York meal, the last, he said to himself, that he might have for many a day.

Therefore he strolled languidly along, with his hands in his pockets, until he reached Third Avenue, and not half a block away he found a small oyster house, in which he thought he could be well fed. In taking a seat at one of the small tables, he called the waiter to him in a lordly manner, that caused the other diners in the room to smile broadly, and bade him bring him a beefsteak, potatoes, a piece of apple pie, and "be quick about it."

"Which will you have first, sir, the pie or the steak," said the waiter with perfect gravity.

"You can bring me de pie, an' I'll eat it while de steak is cookin'," replied Skinny, and was astonished to notice that his remarks were greeted with a general roar of laughter, in which the waiter and cashier, as well as the guests, joined heartily.

Having eaten his dinner, he returned to the depot, easily found his train, and in a very short time was being whirled along over the smooth road that leads to Albany. He had never been twenty miles from the city in his life, and as the train sped on, affording him continual glimpses of the broad Hudson, he wondered how much further the country extended, and whether the whole of the United States was like that part of it which he saw from his car window. The train was still many miles from Albany when the darkness succeeded the twilight, the moon and stars came out, and the little street boy looked down upon the great river that was bathed in moonlight and saw it at its best. After awhile he felt himself growing drowsy, then he stirred himself up on the red plush seat, closed his eyes, and did not open them again until the next morning. When he awoke the car was passing slowly through the street of a town, and Skinny wondered if it could be possible that they were back again in New York, after having completed the circuit of the earth. It was some minutes before he could collect his scattered senses, and then the train stopped, the passengers streamed out, and Skinny learned that they were in Syracuse, and that everybody was going out for breakfast.

Thrusting his hand in his inner pocket he found that his money was still there, and as he entered the big dining-room in the railroad depot, he chuckled to think of the meal that he was going to enjoy at somebody else's expense. It was an ordinary railroad restaurant, and a great many of the well-dressed passengers were turning up their nose at the coffee, which was served in thick china cups, and at the sandwiches, triangles of pie, bits of cold chicken that were displayed on the counter under glass cases, like curiosities in a museum, but the little street boy from New York thought it one of the finest places he had ever been in, and the breakfast which he consumed was certainly superior to anything that he had been accustomed to.

Breakfast over, he strolled out on the platform, and, with his hands in his pockets and his sharp eyes noting everything and everybody that came within their range of vision, he walked up and down whistling in a shrill manner, and creating no small amount of amusement. Having entertained the depot loungers for a few moments, he sought out the Oswego train, climbed aboard it, and just as it was on the point of starting, waved his hand cheerfully to the group who were watching him from the depot. At Oswego he ate another breakfast, and then boarded the train for Rocky Point, a small village on the shore of Lake Ontario.

Chapter XXVI.

AS soon as the train had left Oswego, Skinny took from his pocket the written instructions that Mr. Korwein had given him and devoted a quarter of an hour to a close study of it. Then he put it back in his pocket, consulted a time table of the road and found that there was a station next to Rocky Point and not more than three miles distant from it. At this station the boy determined to alight and perform the remainder of his journey on foot. It would look suspicious, he thought, for a boy of his size and raggedness to arrive in a village by any such luxurious mode of travel as a railroad train. He felt that he would be expected to go at once from the depot to the best hotel in the town and if he started out in quest of a job he would instantly be looked upon by the authorities as a suspicious character. It would be more in keeping with his appearance as well as his purpose to arrive on foot by way of the high road.

Therefore he left the train at the station next the one he was journeying to, and started to finish the distance on foot. It was a cool autumn morning with just enough warmth in the sun's rays to make walking enjoyable. The road which he took afforded him a view of Lake Ontario, as it ran parallel with the shore of that great inland sea. Skinny thought it was salt water; in fact he thought all large bodies of water were salt, and although he soon found himself very thirsty it never occured to him to go down to the beach which in some places was within fifty yards of the road and take a drink. So he trudged patiently along, hoping to find some well or spring, and while he was walking and whistling he was surprised to see lying by the roadside a new red shawl which had evidently been dropped from some passing vehicle. He picked it up instantly for it was his habit to pick up whatever he could find in his way. It was a good shawl of a bright pattern and apparently had not been worn much. Skinny examined it carefully, wondering what use he could make of it. Then he shook his head doubtfully, tucked the shawl under his arm and trudged on as before. He had not gone far before he saw a carriage approaching, and as it drew near he noticed that it was driven by a lady who looked anxiously about her on both sides of the road while she urged her horse rapidly forward. Skinny, who at this moment was enjoying a short rest on a big stone under an oak tree, remarked the lady's appearance and said to himself "Dat must be de one dat lost de shawl."

His first impulse was to conceal it behind the stone upon which he sat, but another idea—one that was more honest and more politic as well —came into his head, and as she was about to drive past him he started up from his seat and called to her, at the same time displaying the red garment in his hand. The lady stopped her horse suddenly and Skinny stepped over to the carriage and said "I found dat shawl up de road, but I guess it's yours."

As he said this he found that he was speaking to a young buxom and healthy woman who looked as if she might be the wife of some prosperous farmer. He saw also that she had been driving very fast, for her horse was panting and wheezing very much after the manner of the horses of New York that were used to bring the afternoon papers from Park Row to the upper part of the city. She looked down at the ragged boy who stood by her wheel with the red shawl thrown over his arm and then she smiled in what the little newsboy thought was a wonderfully sweet and winning way, and still smilling, she said: "Yes that is my shawl. I lost it about three quarters of an hour ago and I was so afraid that somebody would pick it up and make off with it that I just drove back as fast as I could, to get it. Where did you find it?"

"Along dere a little ways" replied the boy indicating with his right hand the direction from which he had come.

"And who are you little boy, and where do you come from?" continued the lady still smiling pleasantly.

"Oh I was just out for a walk," replied Skinny with his accustomed air of careless bravado, but just then he happened to remember the role that he was assuming, and he added with great haste "I taut mebbe I could get a job some'rs around here. I want work, dat's wot I want."

Having said this he politely handed his new acquaintance her shawl and stood regarding her critically through his keen blue eyes. The young lady in her turn subjected the boy to a scrutiny that was as careful as that with which he regarded her and in a moment or two she said "If you will get into the carriage with me I will take you down to my house and perhaps my husband will find something for you to do.

At any rate, he will give you something for finding the shawl."

"I don't want nuthin' for lettin' go de shawl. I wanter get a job of some kind ernuther. I tink I'd like ter try a little country life."

"Well, jump in with me and I'll see what can be done for you" rejoined his new acquaintance, and Skinny accepted her invitation without another word. He climbed up to the seat beside her and waited quietly while she turned her horse around and started in the direction of Rocky Point. The boy enjoyed the ride very much, but although it was full of wonderful surprises to him, he did not show by his face or manner that it was the first time in his life that he had ever been more than twenty miles away from New York. As for the broad expanse of water that lay stretched out before him he was sure it was either the Atlantic Ocean or the Gulf of Mexico or the Pacific, he did not know which and he did not care enough to ask. As they rode along they passed field after field of ripened corn and wide orchards in which men were busy shaking the fruit from the trees and gathering it in great heaps on the grass ready for packing in barrels. Occasionally they passed bits of woodland in which the trees, touched by the early frosts, were brilliant in red, yellow and scarlet. Farmers passed them on the road, riding in wagons piled high with corn and apples, and once Skinny saw a load of yellow pumpkins, the like of which he had never set eyes on before. It was all very new and strange to the city boy, and his keen eyes took in everything about him, but not a word escaped his lips that betrayed his utter ignorance of country life.

He made up his mind, however, that it would be best for him to tell his companion that he had come from New York, because, he argued, she would be sure to find it out herself even if she had not already noticed the difference between a boy from the city and the "jayhawkers," as he denominated them whom he judged constituted the bulk of the population of the neighborhood. Therefore he told her that he had made his way from New York by easy stages—"dey wuz easy too" he said to himself with a chuckle—and that he wanted to get work on a farm or in a country hotel. To the lady who rode beside him, the boy's desire to get out of the city into the country seemed but a natural one, while his honesty in restoring her lost shawl and his avowed purpose to get work of some kind commended him strongly to her, and she determined to give him whatever help she could. On the outskirts of the village of Rocky Point she drew up in front of a large, comfortable looking farm house and bade her companion descend and open the gate. A tall, sunburned and bearded man who was standing in his shirt sleeves by the barn door now came forward to greet his wife.

"I've brought a boy home for you Silas," she remarked pointing to Skinny who was standing holding the gate open for her to enter, "what do you think of him?" The husband smiled pleasantly in response but the glance which he bestowed on the new arrival was one of curiosity blended with a degree of suspicion.

"Where did you pick him up," he said as he helped his wife to alight.

It was a strange thing to the newsboy, whose life had been spent in the streets of the great city, to find himself awaking the next morning in a clean, wholesome bed in a room which, if not elegant, was at least comfortable, neat and redolent of old fashioned country herbs. Of course he did not question the honesty of his host or hostess but from sheer force of habit and as a precautionary measure, too, he examined the roll of bills in his inside pocket and assured himself that they were all there.

Then he dressed himself, stole quietly down stairs and found Mrs. Wolcott busy in her big kitchen.

Her husband was out in the barn, and there Skinny found him, giving the horses and cattle their morning meal. There was plenty about the farm for a boy to turn his hand to, and Skinny's first job was driving the cows out to the pasture where there was still to be found a good deal of grass that had defied the cold weather. It was an easy and not unpleasant task strolling along the road, letting down the bars of the pasture lot, watching the cattle as they streamed through, and then putting up the bars and walking back to the farm house where Mrs. Wolcott had just put the breakfast on the table. The boy found, too, that his walk had given him an excellent appetite and he consumed such an amount of country luxuries as fairly surprised himself. Breakfast over he helped the farmer put the two horses in the big wagon, then climbed in and accompanied him to the corn field a mile away.

By the exercise of his customary and habitual silence, and by carefully watching the farmer and the hired man, Skinny managed not only to acquit himself with credit in their eyes but to impress them with the idea, that it might be a handy thing to have a boy of his sort about the farm all the time, or at least until the harvesting was over.

During that day Skinny did more solid work, ate more good food, and breathed more pure air than in any other one day of his career, and when night came he fell asleep and did not stir again until he was aroused by the farmer early in the morning. Then he repeated his experience of the day before, and by the time Sunday came around he had come to the conclusion that country life was not so bad, after all, and that there were worse people in the world than "jayhawkers," as he called them. On Sunday morning, Mr. and Mrs. Wolcott started, in their best clothes, for church, a proceeding which seemed so remarkable to Skinny that he inquired why they went there. They would have taken him with them, too, if his clothes had been more presentable, but although Mrs. Wolcott had made some repairs in his torn jacket, and provided him with a new and clean shirt, he was still unmistakably a ragged New York street boy, and would have been out of place in the village church, where all the country lads were taken, neatly washed and combed, and with their boots well greased and their clothes carefully brushed.

So Skinny remained at home with the hired man, who promptly went to sleep on the hay in the barn, after the fashion of all hired men, leaving the strange boy to his own devices. That was exactly what he wanted, and taking a piece of paper and a pencil from the parlor table, he seated himself in a corner of the kitchen, and addressed the following letter to his employer, at the same time congratulating himself on the diligence which he had displayed at the night school in the Newsboys' lodging-house, which had enabled him to write so freely and elegantly. This was what he had to say:

"MR. KORWEIN—
SIR:—I have got a job on a farm, and will do what you told me when I get the chance. No more at present, from
SKINNY."

The chance which he had been looking for came to him rather unexpectedly that very afternoon, when Mrs. Wolcott asked him to take a letter to the post office for her, and suggested at the same time that he should take a little walk around the village.

"Wot sort uv tings is dere ter see in dis place?" asked the boy.

"Well," replied the other, smiling, "the usual afternoon walk is down over the bridge to the cemetery, and if you keep up along that road a mile further, you'll find some very pretty woods that go down to the shore."

"All right," replied the boy, "I'll take in all de sights."

Stopping at the post-office, he mailed his own letter as well as the other, and then kept on down the village street, across the bridge and up the hill to the old burying-ground, in which a number of rustic couples were enjoying their regular Sunday afternoon stroll. These looked with some surprise and a little amusement, at the ragged boy, who was prowling about from one headstone to the other, reading the panegyrics and inscriptions, and evidently hunting for some particular grave. But although he searched diligently for nearly an hour, he could find no gravestone that answered the description given him by Mr. Korwein, and, fearing that he was attracting more attention than he desired, he started to leave, with the intention of returning at some future day, when to his intense surprise, he heard his name called in a familiar voice, and on looking up saw some one whom he knew rapidly approaching him.

Like other boys of his class, born and brought up in the streets of New York, and accustomed from the earliest period of infancy to take part in the great struggle of life, Skinny possessed a degree of stoicism that would have done credit to an Indian warrior, and it was seldom, indeed, that he was taken off his guard, no matter what happened. But this time his surprise was so great that he forgot himself, and standing stark still in the path, exclaimed "Hully gee!"

The next moment Bruce Decker was wringing him by the hand, and saying: "What in the world brings you up here?"

Skinny grinned broadly, and replied: "I'm a haymaker now, workin' on a farm here. Dere's lots to eat, and a good place to sleep. I tink I'll stay here all winter. But I taut you wuz in New York."

This is the town I used to live in when I was a small boy," replied Bruce, "and I've just come back here for a short visit. This is the first time I've been here since I went into the fire department, and it's great to get out in the country again. But when did you leave the city? I wanted to see you, and I went down to that lodging-house, but you were not there. I was afraid I wouldn't run across you again."

"I s'pose yer taut that I wuz goin' ter sneak wid dat money, but I wa'nt. I'm earnin' it up here."

"My mother is buried here."—*Page 248.*

"Never mind about that money," rejoined Bruce hastily. "I wanted to see you about some other things. I wanted to find out some more about that man with the scarred face you told me about who sent you on the errands up to Harlem. Have you seen him since we parted?"

For a moment the other boy hesitated, remembering his instructions to observe secrecy. Then he remembered that he owed his life to Bruce, and that, according to his code, he was bound to him, rather than to a man who was nothing more than his employer. "Yes," he said, hesitatingly, "I seen him de odder day, but he didn't say nuthin' about you."

No, of course he wouldn't," answered Bruce, "and I don't want you to say anything to him about me, either, but for all that, I want to get on his track and find out who he is, just for reasons of my own, and as soon as I get back to the city I want you to take me where I can find him."

Skinny made no reply, but continued to regard the other with his keen, light-blue eyes, and then Bruce went on in softer tones: "My mother is buried here, and I came out to see her grave. Come over here, and I'll show it to you." Leading the way, across an empty bit of grass, he stopped in front of a small gray headstone, and there the New York street boy read a name which caused him to forget himself for the second time that afternoon, and to exclaim once more "Hully gee!"

Never, up to that moment, had he in any way connected Bruce, whom he knew only by his first name, with the mission on which he had been sent, but now a sudden gleam of comprehension lit up his mind, for he saw on the gravestone before him the inscription:

SACRED TO THE MEMORY

OF

MARY, WIFE OF FRANK DECKER,

BORN DEC. 1ST, 1855,

DIED SEPT. 5TH, 1877.

Chapter XXVII

LET us return now to the Van Kuren family, whom we last saw at the moment of their departure for Europe. Mr. Van Kuren having determined to give himself a long rest and his children opportunities for travel in foreign lands and study under the most competent instructors, journeyed at once to Paris and there established himself in a great hotel intending to take a place in the suburbs of the French capital. Laura and her brother amused themselves by walking and riding through the city, sometimes with their aunt and sometimes with Mr. Reed, their tutor, but there were many hours which they were compelled to spend in their rooms engaged in study, for their lessons went on under the supervision of their tutor just exactly as they had at home.

One morning they were sitting together in the parlor of Mr. Van Kuren's apartment talking about America and their many friends there, as they frequently did, and Bruce's name came up with the others.

"I wish," said Laura, "that papa would let us write to him, because he must think it very strange that he has heard nothing from us since we went away. You see he knows nothing about us or why we had to break off our friendship so suddenly."

"Oh I'll get around papa all right one of these days," said Harry carelessly, "and I've no doubt he'll let me send him a letter when I ask him to."

They were still talking about Bruce and wondering whether he had completely recovered from his injuries, when the door opened and their father entered in company with a white haired gentleman whom they recognized at once as the one who had occupied the big house near their own and whose name they had long since been forbidden to mention. They looked up now with their eyes wide open with surprise, as their father called to them by name and said, "Samuel, these are my children. You haven't seen them since they were very small." Mr. Dexter extended his hand and said with an extremely pleasant smile on his pale face, "Yes I remember them very well. This is Laura and this is Harry. You don't remember me, children, I suppose?"

Laura made no reply, but Harry spoke up in his impulsive, boyish way and said, "why you're the gentleman who lives in that, big square house, and used to come and see us ever so many years ago, I remember you well but papa told us long ago that we mustn't—"

"That will do Harry," said his father hastily and in a stern tone of voice which his son was thoroughly familiar with. Then he turned to Mr, Dexter and said, "It's some years since we've seen you and I didn't think the boy had such a good memory."

"Yes," replied the other, who had been amused at Harry's interrupted remark, "a fatally good memory, I see. But how long do you intend to stay in Paris?"

"A month or so" said Mr. Van Kuren, and then the children were sent out of the room and he and Mr Dexter seated themselves and entered into a long talk which lasted until the time came for dinner. During that meal, of which Mr. Dexter partook also, he asked both Harry and Laura a great many questions about their studies and amusements, and evinced an interest in them which neither could quite understand. Laura was burning to tell him all about Bruce aud his strange recollection of the old house, but no opportunity offered itself, and soon after dinner Mr. Dexter went out with her father, leaving the brother and sister to amuse themselves until bed-time.

That night Laura made up her mind to speak to Mr. Dexter as soon as possible about the subject that was uppermost in her mind. She longed to ask her father or her aunt why it was that this old gentleman, whom they had been brought up to avoid, should suddenly appear before them in Paris as her father's friend and guest, but when on the following day she ventured to broach the subject, she was told so peremptorily that little children should not ask questions, that she did not venture to repeat her attempt, but determined to await an opportunity to speak to Mr. Dexter himself. That opportunity soon offered itself, for the old gentleman became a frequent visitor at the hotel, calling upon her father almost every day and either going out with him or else remaining for long and close conversations. Miss Van Kuren went with them in their journeys or joined them in their talk, but it was some days before Laura found the chance for which she was looking so anxiously.

One morning the old gentleman arrived just after the whole of the Van Kuren family, excepting Laura, had gone out and it was she therefore who received him in the private parlor. Mr. Dexter seated himself in an easy chair by the fire and entered into conversation with the young girl regarding her lessons, her friends in America and the amusement which she found in Paris. This was the chance she had been waiting for, and with an air of deep mystery she said.

"Mr Dexter there was a very curious thing that happened some time ago and if I tell you I want you to promise me not to say anything about it to anybody not even to papa, and particularly not to Harry." In her eagerness she forgot the agreement she had made with Bruce, an agreement which had more than once prevented him from speaking of the subject to friends and others who might have aided him in his search.

"Certainly my dear, I will make that promise" replied Mr. Dexter, with a benificent smile, "now tell me what this mysterious thing is. I assure you I am very anxious to know."

Then Laura told him the story with which my readers have been already made familiar—she described to him their acquaintance with Bruce and repeated what he had told her in regard to the old house and his instant recognition of it. As she proceeded, the old gentleman's interest in her story grew stronger and stronger, and when she ended he wiped the perspiration from his forehead with a hand that was by no means steady and exclaimed "What you tell me is very strange indeed! I remember the young man very well. He came up to my house one day to get some magazines and papers that I had there; and so he found Harry that very day did he? Well my dear, I scarcely know what to think of it, for strangely enough his story fits in with certain other things that I have learned within a year and makes it more than possible that—but after all what is the use of allowing such thoughts to enter my head?" and breaking off abruptly he rose from his chair pacing slowly up and down the floor talking indistinctly to himself as he did so.

And as he walked, Laura, who had become thoroughly excited over the mystery which she found as romantic and interesting as any she had ever found in a novel, watched him intently, carefully noting the effect that her words had had on him and wondering what the meaning of the whole matter was.

"Do you happen to know the address of this young man?" inquired Mr. Dexter suddenly stopping in his walk.

"Mr. Dexter * * * held out his hand for the address."—
Page 257.

"Yes," said Laura, "I'll run and get it for you, but you must never tell anybody that I did because it would make awful trouble for me."

When she returned she found her father, her aunt and Harry in the room and for a moment she was at a loss what to do, but Mr. Dexter, who was anxiously looking for her, held out his hand for the address and said, as Laura placed the scrap of paper in it, "Remember, this is our secret, my little girl, and Harry is not to know anything about it."

The way in which he said this and the smile with which his words were accompanied stimulated Harry's curiosity and at the same time served to put the elders off the scent. Then the conversation was turned into other channels and in five minutes the incident had passed out of the minds of everyone but the two concerned in it.

That afternoon Laura spread her writing materials on the parlor table and sat down to write her regular weekly letter to her dear friend in America, Kitty Harriott. She had just written "Dear Kitty," when a thought came into her mind that caused her to drop her pen and sit for a moment in deep meditation. Then with cheeks flushed with excitement, she continued as follows:

"I hope you are well and enjoying yourself and that all the other girls are well too. We are having a splendid time here but we have to study as hard as we did at home. There is something that I want you to do for me and you must never tell any one that I mentioned it to you for it is something very mysterious and important. You know about Bruce Decker, the young fireman who was in the hospital. I have often talked to you about him. Well, Papa has made me promise not to write to him and I dare not disobey him, but I did not promise that you would not write to him, and something has happened which he ought to know. I want you to write him a letter and send it to the address on the scrap of paper enclosed. Tell him that Mr. Dexter and Papa are great friends now and he comes to see us every day. This morning I was alone when he called and he sat down and we had a long talk. I told him what Bruce told me about the Dexter house (just write it that way and he will know what I mean), and he was very much interested in what I said and got up and walked up and down the room talking to himself but I could not hear a word he said. Then he asked me for Bruce's address and I copied it out and gave it to him right before Papa and Aunt Sarah and Harry who had all come into the room, and Harry's wild to know what was on the paper I gave him. Now Kitty you must do exactly what I tell you. Bruce will know who you are because he has heard me talk about you and I'm sure he's just dying to know you. But remember it is important that he should get this message right away and nobody must know anything about it. If he makes any answer to your note write to me at once. No more at present, from

     Your loving friend
     Laura Van Kuren."

Chapter XXVIII.

NOW the interest which old Mr. Dexter had betrayed while listening to Laura's story was in reality as nothing compared with that which he felt, and when he reached his home that afternoon he seated himself by the fire and fell into a condition of deep thought.

Mr. Van Kuren who called on him that evening found him in his parlor busy with a number of old letters, papers and photographs which were spread out on the table before him.

"You see," he said as he rose to greet his guest, "that even here in Paris, with enough to render most men contented, my thoughts go back to my old friends and home in America. I don't know whether I shall ever return or not; but of late I have been thinking seriously of running over to New York for a week or two to settle a little matter of business that has been worrying me for a short time past."

Mr. Dexter did not explain that the "short time past" meant only about eight hours nor did he, of course, say what the matter was that troubled him but his guest divined that it might be some family affair and asked him if that were not the case.

"Well yes," rejoined Mr. Dexter, "it is a family matter, and one that I cannot settle very well by mail, though I might write my nephew and ask him to attend to it for me."

"Your nephew?" exclaimed Mr. Van Kuren, "why I was not aware that you were even on speaking terms with him, and for my part I would not blame you if you never have anything more to say to him."

The older man looked up at his visitor, and said very gently and with the same pleasant smile that always came into his face when he spoke to either Harry or Laura, "My dear Horace, when you reach my age you will be anxious to settle up all your earthly quarrels so that when the time comes for you to leave this world you may do so with a feeling that you leave no enemies behind."

"But do you mean to tell me," demanded Mr. Van Kuren, "that you have become a friend of that good-for-nothing nephew of yours again? I can't understand it after the way in which he treated you ten years ago."

"You must remember, Horace, that Sam is the only blood relation I have left in this world. He came to see me a few months before I left

America, and I found him so regretful for the past, and so much changed for the better that I have now fully as much confidence in him as I ever had in my own son."

Mr. Van Kuren shrugged his shoulders, and after a moment's hesitation, replied, "There's nothing in the world that would induce me to place any confidence whatever in Sam Dexter, even if he is your only blood relation. It is entirely through him that the misunderstanding occurred which separated us for years, and I have heard of him in New York of late as connected with some very dubious enterprises."

"But my dear Horace," continued the old gentleman, "you must not believe everything that you hear. I have no doubt that my nephew's career has not been altogether what it should have been; but that he is thoroughly contrite now I have no reason to doubt. When he first came to see me I supposed, of course, that he was in want of money again, and was therefore inclined to be a little suspicious, but when he not only assured me, but proved to me, that he had a handsome sum laid by out of his savings for a future day, that he wanted nothing of me, and was only anxious to heal up old breaches while I was still alive, then I was forced to admit that he was, indeed, a different man from the one whom I had known formerly."

"Do you mean to say that he never tried to beg or borrow anything from you, that is to say, since this last reconciliation?" demanded Mr. Van Kuren, incredulously.

"I certainly do mean to say exactly that," replied the other emphatically. "He is occupying the old house at present but that is because I asked him to do so. It is not safe to leave one's home in the hands of servants or caretakers."

Mr. Van Kuren shrugged his shoulders again and remarked, in a tone that showed he had no faith in the repentance or sincerity of Mr. Dexter's nephew: "Well, just mark my words, that man will still manage to injure you in some way. He is not to be trusted."

For a few moments the old gentleman sat quietly looking into the fire, then he lifted his eyes and said, "I should be sorry to have as bad an opinion of Sam as you have, but it may be that you are nearer right in your estimate of him than I am. Nevertheless it's an old man's fancy, and one that should be, for that reason, pardoned, to feel that after he is gone he will be succeeded at his home and in his estate by one of his own blood rather than by a stranger."

"And so," remarked Mr. Van Kuren dryly, "you have arranged to make Sam your heir, have you?"

"Yes that is my present intention. As my will stands now, all my property goes to my son and as he is dead, Sam as the next of kin would inherit it anyway, Therefore I hardly think it necessary to write a new one, but will destroy the old one, which will throw the property into his hands."

"And does he know this?" asked Mr. Van Kuren.

"I haven't told him so in so many words, but I am sure he must know what my intentions are. However he has never broached the topic to me and I am bound to say that he seems to be thoroughly disinterested in his regard for me."

"In that case," observed Mr. Van Kuren, watching his friend's face carefully as he spoke, "you had better write to him and ask him to arrange this little family matter that troubles you. At any rate it will save you the trouble of making a trip across the water. A journey at your time of life and at this season of the year might be regarded as almost unsafe."

Mr. Dexter made no reply to this remark, and there was silence in the room for fully a minute. Then he shook his head slowly, and said: "No, I don't exactly like to ask Sam to help me in this affair, and perhaps, after all it would be better for me to write than to make the journey myself."

"My dear Mr. Dexter," said Mr. Van Kuren, rising from his seat and placing his hand on his old friend's arm, "the mere fact that you do not write to him in this matter is a proof that you do not fully trust him; but don't take the trip yourself. Write a letter; this is no season for a man of your age to travel."

Soon after this the visitor took his leave, and the old gentleman sat down at his library table and addressed a polite and formal note to Bruce Decker, telling him what he had learned from a mutual friend, and asking him to send him full information concerning himself and his family, adding that he very well remembered meeting him before, and hoped that he was making progress in the calling which he had chosen. Having sealed and addressed this letter he sat for some time lost in reflection. Then taking up his pen again, he wrote another letter to the man to whom Mr. Van Kuren had referred as "Sam."

Both these letters reached New York on the same day, and were the cause of the strange meeting of the two boys, which has been described in another chapter. But in the letter to his kinsman, Sam, the old gentleman did not reveal the address which Laura had given him.

Chapter XXIX.

WHEN Skinny the Swiper, standing in the little country burying-ground, looked upon the time-stained marble slab, and deciphered the inscription upon it, he opened his eyes in wonder, and for the second time within five minutes, uttered the exclamation which he kept on hand for such emergencies as demanded something more vigorous and expressive than commonplace English.

"Hully gee!" was all that this little New York street boy had to say; but coming from him it possessed a deeper significance than is conveyed by the cold type which spells the words.

First he looked at the grave stone, and then he looked at Bruce Decker, and finally he asked: "Wuz dat your mother?"

"Yes," replied Bruce, simply.

Skinny said nothing but he thought a great deal; and while he was thinking he scratched his head and looked down at the half obliterated mound of earth that marked the grave of Mrs. Decker. From the very first he had suspected that there was some connection between the gallant young fire laddie, who had saved his life and carried him from the burning building, and the scarred and bearded man who had sent him to this remote corner of the world. He had not forgotten that he had been solemnly charged not to breathe a word to any human being in regard to his strange errand, and he had an intuitive feeling that if he violated in any way the trust reposed in him, his employer would learn of it, and mete out to him a terrible vengeance, instead of the liberal reward that he had promised.

On the other hand, he saw before him the boy who had done for him what no one else in the world would have done for a friendless, ragged child of the streets, and for a moment he hesitated as to which of these two masters he should choose to serve. To the one he owed a certain amount of loyalty—a few dollars worth, perhaps—but to the other he owed his life. He raised his eyes, and encountered the clear, honest, truthful ones of Bruce, which looked him square in the face, and he hesitated no longer. Rough contact with the world had taught him to be suspicious of others, and it was rare enough in his career that he had encountered any one whom he fully trusted. But there was that in Bruce's face which caused him to say to himself: "Dat man is all right, an' white," which is a high compliment for a newsboy to pay any one.

Having reached the conclusion that Bruce was the best friend he was likely to have in the world, he took from his pocket the written instructions which Mr. Korwein had given him, handed the paper to the new master whom he had elected to serve, and blurted out: "Hay, boss, ain't dat de same party?"

To say that Bruce was surprised when he saw his mother's name written in an unknown handwriting, and in the possession of his little hospital friend but feebly describes his condition of mind.

"Come over here with me," he said, as he led the way to a low stone wall, somewhat remote from the couples who were walking up and down the paths, laughing and whispering and talking. Then, seating himself on a convenient bowlder, he said to Skinny: "How in the world did you ever get hold of this paper?"

And Skinny in reply told him the whole story of the dark-bearded man, who had summoned him to his office, and sent him away to the shore of the great inland lake, simply to get information about Mary Decker and her son, if son she had. Skinny's recital occupied nearly a quarter of an hour, for he stretched it so as to include his adventures while on the road from New York, and the circumstances which had led to his becoming what he called a haymaker. Bruce listened intently to every word the boy uttered, and questioned him narrowly in regard to Mr. Korwein and his motive in entrusting him with such a strange commission. Of course Skinny could not account for the man's motives, and, indeed, that was something he had not troubled himself about. It was enough to him that his employer wished to obtain certain information, and was willing to pay for it So long as he could be well paid for his work he did not concern himself about people's motives, or ask what would be done with the information which he supplied. But he did not neglect to mention the fact that in telling as much as he had, he had betrayed his employer, and he warned his friend to keep strictly to himself all that he had told him. Bruce readily agreed to this, and then, as the afternoon had already merged into twilight, they returned to the village, Skinny, passing on to Mr. Wolcott's house and Bruce going to that of the friends whom he was visiting.

The following evening the two boys met again by agreement, and, with his friend's assistance, Skinny composed and sent to his employer in New York the following letter:

"Mr. Korwein—
Dear Sir:—I went up to the cemetery yesterday, and seen the grave, which had on it

Sacred to the memory
of
Mary, wife of Frank Decker.
Born Dec. 1st, 1855,
Died Sept. 5th, 1877.

Theae wasn't no other graves of any folks named Decker. I am still on the farm. No more at present. From
Skinny."

Then he entrusted to Bruce his employer's address and bade him good-bye with a parting injunction not to let the man know where he learned of him; and with this address in his pocket, Bruce climbed aboard a New York train, said good-bye to a number of admiring villagers who accompanied him to the depot and was borne away toward New York, while the street boy walked slowly back to the Wolcott's.

As the train rolled swiftly along our young hero sat with his face pressed against the car window looking out into the quiet night and thinking over the strange things that happened to him of late. To begin with, there was this dark bearded man of mystery who, he was positive, could tell him everything that he wished to know; and who was this ragged newsboy whom he had befriended—could it be possible that he was simply a hireling of the other a d tnat he had been sent to Rocky Point to sp y pon him? No, he could not doubt Skinny's s ncerity, and the feeling had been growing daily within him that through him the mystery which enveloped his early days and even his origin would finally be cleared up. One thing he had determined, and that was that as soon as he reached New York he would go to Mr. Korwein and boldly ask him—what? That was the trouble. What should he ask him? He would feel very foolish saying to that scarred and bearded gentleman : " Please sir will you tell me who I am and clear up the mystery which enshrouds me ? "

His mind was still busy with this problem when the monotonous motion of the train got the better of his senses and he fell into a deep sleep.

And just at that moment Skinny the Swiper was lying wide awake in the comfortable attic room in which Mr. Wolcott had installed him and was asking himself what it all meant. Why should Mr. Korwein have sent him up to

Rocky Point, and what had he to do with the grave of the young fireman's mother? For the life of him he could not make it out and then he wondered if Mr. Korwein would ever find out about his treachery and at the thought of that great man's wrath he curled himself up in bed, drew the clothes up over his face and resolved that he would remain on the farm until he had changed beyond all recognition. "Anyway," he said to himself, "dis is a better place dan de Bowery, because dere's more to eat an' a place to sleep."

And then he too fell asleep and did not waken until the daylight was streaming through the window over his head and Mrs. Wolcott calling to him from the foot of the stair-case.

The little newsboy found life so pleasant during the autumnal weather on the shore of Lake Ontario that he began to think seriously of settling down to an agricultural life. The air was fine and bracing, the food plentiful and nutritious aud the farmer and his wife treated him with great kindness and did not ask him to do more than a boy's amount of work. Skinny's life had been a hard one, and never in his recollection had he had as much to eat or enjoyed himself more than he had since his arrival in the little country place on the shore of the

great lake. Good treatment was something that was more of a novelty to him than kicks and curses, and when his naturally suspicious mind grasped the fact that the farmer and his wife were kind to him, not because they expected to get the better of him in any way, but because it was their nature to be kind to all living things, and that they trusted him implicitly and seemed inclined to trust him so long as he proved worthy, it occurred to him for almost the first time in his life that there were some people in the world who did not go about with their hands lifted against such Arabs as himself, and he determined to repay their confidence with absolute fidelity to their interests.

He had remained with them nearly a month, and, as has been said already was beginning to think favorably of an agricultural life when something occurred which drove all ideas of rural felicity out of his mind and sent him adrift in the world once more. The something which served to alter his intentions was a letter which came to him one morning in the mail. It was from Bruce Decker who wanted to know how much longer he intended to stay in the country, and whether he could be induced to make a little trip to the city for the purpose of rendering him (Bruce) an important service.

As the newsboy finished spelling out his friend's epistle, a gleam of delight came into his freckled face. Here was another friend who treated him like a human being and came to him as to some one whom he could trust to render him a service. Thrusting the letter into the inside pocket of his jacket he buttoned that faded and rather rusty garment tightly about him and went at once to his employer.

"Say, boss, I gotter go ter de city ter night," was the way in which Skinny announced his intended departure.

"To-night!" exclaimed the farmer, who was accustomed to slow country ways rather than to Skinny's metropolitan swiftness of action, "What's the matter? Don't we use you right?"

"Use me right? Why, boss, der aint nobody never used me no whiter den you an' de missus, but I've gotter go on important bizness an' if yer'll lemme come back when de biz is done, I'll stop wid yer till I'm a reg'lar haymaker."

The farmer saw that the boy was in earnest, and although both he and his wife were sorry to have him go they made no attempt to dissuade him, but fitted him out with a new hat and shoes, and then to the lad's intense surprise handed him a five-dollar note as a present.

"Wot's dis fur?" he demanded, looking with his keen, suspicious little blue eyes from the greenback in his hand to the farmer's ruddy and honest face. He had agreed to work for his keep and never before in his experience had any one of his numerous employers paid him a nickel more than he was obliged to.

"You've earned it, my boy," said the farmer heartily, "and if you want to come back again you'll find a home for you here the same as before. You've saved me hiring an extra man since you have been here and next summer if you choose to pitch in and work the same as you have this fall, I'll do better by you than this."

Skinny was a boy of but few words, but sometimes he did a good deal of quiet thinking. He said but little in farewell to his friends, but as he was passing through the gate he turned for a last look at the house which had given him shelter and at the farmer and his wife who were still standing in the doorway and who had treated him with so much kindness.

The night train bore him swiftly to New York and by nine o'clock the next morning he was standing in front of the superintendent of the Newsboys' Lodging House, in negotiation for what he described as "first-class commerdations widder best grub in der place."

Having made arrangements for food and lodging, the boy started uptown with the intention of seeing Bruce at the truck quarters, but he had not gone many blocks before he felt a strong hand on his shoulder and heard a stern voice behind him saying : " And so you've turned up again, you young rascal! Now, let's hear what you have to say for yourself!"

The newsboy knew the voice at once. There was no need for him to turn his head. He felt that the hand of fate, in the person of the tall, black-bearded man, had overtaken him. But it was not the first time that the hand of vengeance or justice had fallen upon him, and no one knew better than Skinny that such a grasp is not always a sure one. Without even turning his head or uttering a single sound the boy simply slid out of his jacket, twisted himself free and darted around the nearest corner, leaving his captor standing on the sidewalk with the ragged jacket in his hand and on his face a look of rage that it was well for Skinny's peace of mind that he did not see.

"I'll catch him yet, the young vagabond, and find out what he's been doing all this time!"

muttered the tall man between his teeth as he looked down at the shabby garment which remained in his hand as evidence of the brief captivity and sudden, eel-like escape of Skinny the Swiper. He was about to throw the jacket in the gutter, for it would look odd to be seen carrying it through the crowded streets, when his eye fell upon the corner of an envelope protruding from an inside pocket, and thinking that it might contain a clue to the boy's haunts in the city, he took it out and examined it. It was simply a letter written two days before, but it was the signature of Bruce Decker which arrested the attention of the man who read it and brought a sudden gleam into his eyes.

Chapter XXX.

WHEN Bruce returned to New York after his short vacation in the country, he received such a hearty welcome from every member of the company, that he realized the fact that it is a good thing for one to go away now and then if only to indicate the value of one's services.

He had not only enjoyed himself during his absence and gained new health and strength from the clear lake air but he had also proved to the chief and his subordinates that he was a decidedly useful boy. The many little duties which he performed about the quarters had been done so quietly and unostentatiously as well as effectively that it was not until he was out of the city that the others realized how much trouble he saved them. As it was, the men had to burden their minds with a number of small details which had previously been left entirely in Bruce's hands, and every time that one of them was called upon to feed the horses or perform some small duty for the chief he thought of Bruce and wondered how much longer that boy was going to stay away.

On his return he found awaiting him a letter bearing no signature and written in an unformed, girlish hand telling him what he already knew about the interest which Mr. Dexter had felt in him, and although there was nothing in the note to indicate its origin, Bruce knew that it must have been inspired by Laura herself. And a very delightful thing it was to believe that this young girl had taken so much trouble on his account as to ask somebody in America to give him this information. But why did she not write to him herself? That is what puzzled him, for of course he knew nothing about Mr. Van Kuren's reason for breaking off the intimacy.

He had scarcely recovered from the glow of satisfaction which suffused him, as he read his anonymous letter, and thought of the young girl to whose kindly interest he owed it, when Chief Trask approached him and informed him that he was to sleep in the quarters with the men in future, in order to be on hand in case of a night alarm.

"You see, my boy, you're growing older every day now, and I want you to learn this business through and through, so as to be ready to take a man's place when the time comes."

And, in accordance with the Chief's orders, which he was only too glad to obey, Bruce established himself in the dormitory above the truck quarters, and as he placed his head on the pillow that night, and saw that his turn-out was lying on the floor beside him, he realized that, although his name was not on the pay-roll of the department, he was really a fireman at last, and would be expected to respond to an alarm as readily as any of the men in the company.

The next morning as soon he had finished feeding the horses, and attended to the other small duties required of him, he took his particular friend, Charley Weyman, aside and told him of his experiences in the little graveyard at Rocky Point. He told him how Skinny had been sent there by the man whom the newsboy called "Scar-faced Charley," and who was, he was positive, none other than the mysterious stranger that Charley Weyman himself had first told him about.

At the mention of this man, Weyman's face assumed an expression of intense interest, which deepened as Bruce continued with his account of how Skinny had been employed to visit the grave in the little burying ground and ascertain if possible the whereabouts of any living member of the Decker family.

"And so this ugly-faced chap is taking all this trouble to find out whether you were ever borned, and if so, whether you are alive or dead?" exclaimed the fireman. "Well, if it's worth anything to him to find out about you, my opinion is that it's worth just as much to you to find out why he is so much interested. He was just as much concerned about your father that's dead and gone, and he don't seem inclined to lose sight of the family. If I were you, I'd lose no time in finding out what it all means. But let me tell you one thing, that fellow never brought good luck to anybody. Your father was never the same man after he had a visit from him, and if you get him coming around here after you, you may have cause to be sorry for it."

"You know he's living in the same house where I went to call on Mr. Dexter" said Bruce, "and I've been thinking of going up there to pay him a visit and put it to him fair and square, 'what do you want of me, and why are you so interested in the Decker family?'"

For a moment, Weyman remained silent, evidently thinking over what the boy had said to him. Then he made answer: "Yes I think on the whole that's the quickest and surest way of finding out what you want to know. There's nothing like suddenly facing a man of that sort and putting your question to him before he has time to frame some answer that might suit his own purpose. Likely as not if he knew you were coming he'd cook up some reply that would throw you off your scent but when you come upon him unexpectedly he is apt to tell the truth even when it's contrary to his usual practice. Yes I'd go up there if I were you because if he's hunting up for the son of Frank Decker he's bound to come across him sooner or later. It's funny he never came around here to ask the Chief or any of us about him, and it's just as strange to me that he didn't find out at headquarters that you were drawing a pension. However, I've noticed that these very smart and tricky fellows often over-reach themselves by trying to be too smart when they might accomplish something by being straightforward and honest."

Bruce, having slept on the matter, determined to take his friend's advice, and although it was more difficult for him to obtain leave of absence now that he had become a more useful member of the company than formerly, he soon found an opportunity to make the long journey to the upper part of the city where Mr. Dexter's house was situated. Leaving the elevated railroad, he walked a few blocks out of his way in order to pass the gate of the great mansion in which Harry and Laura Van Kuren had lived The house was closed now, aud it was evident from the unkept appearance of the lawn and shrubbery that it's master had been away for some time.

For several minutes he stood leaning sadly upon the gate and thinking of the kind friends whom he had known there, and from whom he was now separated not only by the trackless waste of ocean, but also by something he knew not what, but which was nevertheless an invisible and impassable barrier, It was with a sad heart that he finally turned his back on the Van Kuren mansion and walked rapidly along the same highway which he had last trodden in company with the Van Kuren children and their tutor on that day when he discovered that Mr. Dexter had departed for Europe.

Once more he entered the broad gate and made his way along the winding road through the dense shrubbery to the door of the stately old colonial mansion. A servant answered his ring of the bell and said in response to his inquiry that Mr. Korwein lived there nominally but spent most of his time down town, the woman did not know where. Sometimes she did not see him for a week, and then he would appear suddenly, remain with them three or four days without quitting the house, and then disappear to be gone perhaps a week or two longer. She had no idea where his office was and did not know when Mr. Dexter would return. Having vouchsafed this information, she closed the door, and as her young visitor departed, he heard the bolt sharply snap behind him.

Before leaving the grounds, Bruce walked to the corner of the house and refreshed his memory with another long look at the old vine-clad porch which had attracted his attention on the occasion of his first visit and had suggested to his mind the long search upon which he was still engaged. There it was just as when he had last seen it, just as it was when he saw it in those long gone by childish days.

He returned in a rather disconsolate mood to the quarters and told Weyman the result of his visit.

"Never mind," said the latter, "you mustn't expect to learn every thing all in a hurry. Go up again there the next time you can get away for an afternoon and you may find him. Anyhow while there's life there's hope, and if you can't find him there you may run across him down town some time. Keep your eyes open whenever you go about the streets, and you'll find him some day when you'll least expect him. I never go out without looking for him myself."

Bruce paid two more visits to the Dexter mansion without learning anything further, and it was then that he sat down and wrote the letter to Skinny asking him how soon he expected to be back in town again, the effect of which has been shown in a preceding chapter.

Chapter XXXI.

ABOUT one hour after the brief but violent sidewalk encounter already described, a small and ragged street boy entered Chief Trask's quarters, cast a searching eye over the group of men who were assembled there, and then walked quickly over to Bruce Decker, who was at work, can in hand, oiling the wheels of the chief's wagon.

"Is dis your name, boss?" he inquired, as he handed to him a letter, enclosed in a dirty yellow envelope, on which was written, in sprawling, uncertain characters, the words:

BRUCE DECKER,
In Care of Hook and Ladder.

The young fire lad opened the message, and deciphered the following sentence:

"Cum down and meet me at Lyonse's, and eat supper to-night. Wot time will you come?   SKINNY."

"Dere's an answer ter dat," said the boy, as Bruce finished reading the note.

"Very well, then, tell him I'll be with him at six," he said, and the young ragamuffin departed, while Bruce resumed his work on the chief's wagon, amazed and delighted to get an answer in such a short time to his letter. The afternoon seemed to pass very slowly, and at half-past five he obtained the chief's permission to go out for a little while, and bent his steps immediately to Lyons's, a restaurant on the Bowery, which Skinny visited once in a while when he was prosperous enough to treat himself to a substantial meal.

Bruce found the little newsboy standing in front of the open door.

"I got your note yesterday, an' here I am," was Skinny's greeting, as the two boys shook hands. "I cum right on de minute I knowed I wuz wanted here," he added, "an' what's more I've got dat mun' yer let me have de time we cum outter de hospital," and he handed four dollars and twenty-two cents to his companion, with a distinct look of pride.

It pleased Bruce very much to feel that his humble little friend was so honest and so willing to do his bidding, and he said so in a hearty, straightforward manner that Skinny readily understood. Then they entered the restaurant, selected a quiet table, in an obscure corner, and sat down to a nice supper, Skinny acting as host for perhaps the first time in his life. And as they ate they talked, the newsboy describing his experiences on the farm, and Bruce plying him with questions about the different country people he knew.

Never before in his life had Bruce felt so much like a character in a story book as he did now, and even Skinny remarked that the situation reminded him of a similar one in his favorite romance "Shorty, the Boy Detective."

It was the first time that the newsboy had ever entertained anyone at a dinner as sumptuous as the one which he now offered to the young lad whom he admired and liked as he liked and admired no other human being. He recommended all the most expensive dishes on the bill of fare, ordered the waiter around in a way that brought a broad smile to that functionary's face, and "showed off" in so many other ways that Bruce, who was at heart a modest and unobtrusive young chap, finally felt constrained to ask him to attract less attention, and conduct himself with more decorum.

The fact was, that Skinny "felt his oats" as they say in the country. He was very proud to be called in as a sort of advisory counsel in such a delicate and important matter as the one which now occupied Bruce's mind, and he was ready enough to give his friend the full benefit of his long experience in the city and really remarkable knowledge of the habits of crooked, crafty and dangerous people. Young as he was, the newsboy had long since learned the great lesson of eternal vigilance, and he knew well enough that the man whom he called "Scar-faced Charlie" was not one in whom implicit confidence should be reposed.

He listened attentively as Bruce described his visits to the Dexter mansion, and then said to him "Wot's de matter wid bracin' him in his Eldridge Street joint?"

"But I don't know where it is" replied the other.

"Come along wid me, an' I'll show yer" said Skinny quickly, and, having paid the check and handed the amazed waiter a quarter, coupling his gift with an admonition to "hustle lively" the next time he had any visitors of distinction to wait on, the newsboy led the way down the Bowery which was by this time crowded with people and brilliantly lighted, to Grand Street, and then in an easterly direction to a corner from which he could see the building in which Mr. Korwein had his office.

But beyond this corner Skinny positively refused to go. Plucky as he was, and heedless

of results, he had a profound fear for the big strong man out of whose stern grasp he had wriggled that very day.

"You go over dere, an' brace de old bloke. I'll wait here. He's dere, fer de light's in the windy," he said. And Bruce was forced to make his visit alone.

Never before in his life had he gone about any task that so tried his nerves as this one, and it was fully five minutes before he could make up his mind to open the door and enter the money-lender's dingy office. At last, however, his will conquered his fears, and he marched boldly up the steps, opened the door and closed it behind him with a sharp bang. Mr. Korwein was standing behind the tall desk adding up a long column of figures in his ledger. He looked up as the boy entered and said rather roughly: "Well, what can I do for you this evening?"

"I'm not quite sure what you can do for me" rejoined his visitor, looking him carefully in the face and speaking in a tone which arrested the tall man's attention at once. "I heard that you are making some rather particular inquiries about me, and I thought if there was anything you wanted to know, I might be able to tell you myself."

"Inquiries about you!" repeated Mr. Korwein, dropping his pen and coming out from behind the tall desk, in order to get a good view of his visitor, "why, who are you?"

"My name is Bruce Decker, and I am the son of Frank Decker, the fireman" was the boy's answer.

Not much in the words he uttered nor in the tone of his voice, one would say. But enough to drive every particle of color from the money-lender's face and to cause him to start back with a half suppressed oath on his lips, and an expression in which rage, disappointment and astonishment seemed to be blended in equal parts.

"Frank Decker's son! He never had any son!" he exclaimed.

Oh yes he did," replied Bruce" and I am that son. I heard you were looking for me. Now that I am here, tell me what you want."

"And so you are really Frank's boy are you" said the money-lender, speaking in a more conciliatory tone and evidently trying to recover his equanimity, "well I am glad to see you, glad to see you. I've been looking for you because, because—to tell the truth, there is a little money coming to you, not much my boy, not very much, but something. It was left to your father, and by his death goes to his next of kin. If you are really his son, you are entitled to it. But I must have proof you know, proof, before I can pay it over. Where do you live, my boy? Let me know your address and I will look you up and see that you recieve every cent that is your due." He wiped the perspiration from his face as he entered with much care in a memorandum book the address which Bruce gave him, which was that of Chief Trask's house and not of the boy's. And then, declaring that he conld say no more until he recieved absolute proof that Bruce was what he represented himself to be, he opened the door and ushered his visitor out into the street.

Bruce stood for a moment on the sidewalk, utterly bewildered by what he had heard.

"Well, did yer brace de bloke?" demanded Skinny appearing suddenly in front of him,

"Yes," answered Bruce "and he told me he had some money to pay me that was left to my father,"

"Hully gee" exclaimed the boy. "Better look out though dat yer get all wot's comin' to yer Dat Scar-faced Charlie don't never pay bills in full."

Chapter XXXII

IN his private office in the poor, shabby building, in which for reasons best known to himself he had chosen to establish his place of business, the tall saturnine black bearded and altogether mysterious character known already to some of our readers sat busy with books and letters.

In the outer office his bookkeeper stood at his tall desk pausing now and then to talk to those who came in, intent on some business errand, and once in a while referring some particular person to his master who sat in the inside room.

It was just twelve o'clock and during the morning all sorts of people had been coming and going in and out of that dingy little place of business. Some of the visitors were well to do in appearance while others looked as if poverty and misfortune had long since claimed them as their own. Some were men and others women, and there were three or four children among the clients of the place. If the visitors were noticeable for any one thing it was for the stealthy and mysterious manner in which they entered and made known their wishes to the bookkeeper who stood guard at the outer office. This functionary, by the way, seemed to be well acquainted with nearly every one that called, and he usually had a word of greeting that was sometimes pleasant sometimes sarcastic and often contemptuous. To a man with a cast in his eye who slouched cautiously in after having scanned the neighborhood from under his hat for at least three minutes before entering, the bookkeeper said jocosely:

"Well what have you got for us to-day? Any nice loose diamonds or a few watch cases?"

"Hush!" exclaimed the visitor warily as he laid his finger against his nose, "you're always talking foolishly. Can I have a word with the boss to-day?"

"I guess so; you're a pretty good customer here. So you may walk right in." The visitor tip-toed into the private room, closed the door behind him, drew his chair up beside the tall saturnine man who was still busy with his pen, and whispered something in his ear that caused him to sit bolt upright and gaze sharply and with amazement in the face of his visitor. For fully an hour the man with the cast in his eye remained in the inner office and when he finally withdrew, the other accompanied him to the door and stood for a moment talking earnestly to him in a low voice before he permitted him to depart. Then he went back to his desk, and his face as he passed through the room, was so stern and troubled that one or two visitors who were seated awaiting his pleasure viewed him carefully, then shook their heads and departed, preferring to talk to him at some time when they should find him in better humor. As for the visitors they all came with one object in view which was money, for the well dressed man who sat at the desk in the inner office made a business of lending money at exorbitant rates of interest and on all sorts securities.

"But why," some reader might inquire, "should a man of good connections and education embark in such a business and select as his headquarters a dirty cheap office in a poverty stricken part of the town?"

And the reply is that he selected a neighborhood in which he knew money to be a scarce commodity, and which all his clients, the high as well as the low, could visit without fear of detection. As has been already said he had clients of various classes. There was one man, for example, who could be found almost any evening in some fashionable club or drawing-room up town and who, on the very morning of which we write, had spent nearly half an hour in that little private office. This man had debts amounting to $25,000, and a father whose fortune of a million he had reasonable hopes of acquiring in due course of time. But his father was a man of the strictest honor, and the son well knew that if he were to hear of his losses at cards and horse racing he would cut him off without a dollar, and leave all his money to a distant cousin whom he had always detested. Situated as he was, this man found the money-lender of Eldridge Street a most convenient friend, and it was an easy matter for the latter to persuade him that for the use of ten or fifteen thousand dollars in cash with which to appease the most importunate of his creditors, he could well afford to give a note for five times the amount payable after the death of his parent.

"And even now," continued the money lender, shaking his head as he handed him a large roll of bills, "I am taking risks that I ought not to take with you or with anybody else. How do I know that you will outlive your father? How do I know that the old man will leave you anything when he dies? How do I know even that he has got anything to leave, or that having it now he will have it a year hence? These are ticklish times, and if I were a prudent business man, without anything of the speculator in me, I would just hang on to what money I've got, and let you and the rest of them like you shift for yourselves. I've half a mind now," he added, suddenly, as he tightened his grip on the greenbacks, which had not quite passed out of his hand, "to tear your note up and put the money back in my safe." But at this threat his visitor snatched the coveted roll from his hand, placed it in his inside pocket, and buttoning his coat up tightly, exclaimed, "Don't talk to me about the chances you take, Mr. Shylock, when you know perfectly well that I'm good for anything I put my name to, and that it won't be long before you get your own again with a pound of my flesh into the bargain."

It will be seen from this conversation that the mysterious bearded man had a keen eye for business, and as his little shop was full of customers from morning till night, one may readily believe that he made a large income with very little mental or physical exertion on his part.

It was just one o'clock when, having disposed of his visiter with the cast in his eye, the money-lender sat behind his desk with his cigar in his mouth, lost in thought. Something must have troubled him for his brow was ruffled and from time to time an angry blush crept into his cheek. One might have noticed too—had there been any one there to notice him—that he started uneasily at every sound that came from the little outer room and finally when he heard a woman's voice raised in shrill anger he stepped to the door, listened for a moment or so and then come out to see what was the matter. It was an old Irish woman who stood with a package in her hand talking angrily to the bookkeeper.

"An' sure you'll not refuse a poor old woman the loan of a ten dollar note on these little bits of things?" she was saying in a voice that betrayed her peevishness and annoyance.

"Can't give you anything to-day, madam," returned the bookkeeper speaking very positively and then, noticing his employer he added, "There's the boss himself, and he'll tell you the same thing."

But the "boss" had already caught a glimpse of the old Irish woman's face, and to the intense surprise of his subordinate he retreated suddenly into his private room, banged the door after him and then thinking better of his act, opened it wide enough to say in a low and guarded whisper, "Give the old woman what she wants and bring the package in to me. Get her address, too. while you're about it."

The bookkeeper did as he was ordered. And as the old woman wrote her name on the receipt with trembling fingers she uttered: "Now remember, I'll be back for this when my allowance comes. But me friends are coming back from Europe soon and they will never let old Ann Crehan go hungry. They'll all be back, the master and Miss Emma and the two young children and then I'll have everything I want. An' it'll be a sorry day for that hard-hearted spalpeen who forgot the one who took care of him and will let her go to the poorhouse for the want of a few dollars. Sure his fine old uncle would never threat me in that fashion."

As the old woman departed, the clerk took the package into the inner office and laid it before his employer, and the latter before opening the paper shut and bolted the door. He found nothing within but a few thin and worn silver spoons and an old fashioned open-faced gold watch. Inside of the case was the following inscription

> "FOR FIDELITY AND COURAGE
> TO ANN CREHAN
> FROM SAMUEL DEXTER."

Well did that strong, bearded man, whose face, with its deep lines and heavy, overhanging brow, was an index to his passionate, wilful nature, know what that inscription meant. It carried him back in memory to a bright, spring morning, years ago, when this same old woman, whose tottering footsteps had just passed over his threshold, was a servant in the family of his kinsman, Samuel Dexter, with whom he, an orphan boy, had found a home. Well did he recall that day, and the accident through which he might have lost his life had it not been for the courage of the Irish servant, who rushed at the peril of her own life, into a burning building, and snatched from the flames the two children who had been committed to her care.

The fierce red scar across his cheek had remained a vivid reminder of that day, and he remembered how, throughout his youth and early manhood, he had always hated his young kinsman, who had been with him in the flames, but who had escaped without disfigurement. Well, the kinsman had long ago passed to his final reward, and he was living still, with the red scar on his face but half concealed by the thick, stiff beard. He folded up the paper containing the watch and the pieces of silver, and put the package carefully away in his safe.

"It's a lucky thing for me, that the old creature didn't recognize me when I put my head through the door," he said to himself. "I'll have to be more careful in the future about showing myself down here, for one never knows who is going to turn up. Everybody wants money, and there are none too proud to come down here to this dirty street and ask for it. It's a great thing, money, and it's the lack of it that puts all men on the same footing."

Chapter XXXIII.

WHEN one is young and life still seems new and fresh and full of bright, ever-changing hues, a few months seem a long period, and one that often brings with it many changes.

And so the year that the Van Kuren children spent abroad was not without its effect upon them. During that time they had travelled through England, France, Italy and Germany, and, under the guidance of their father and their tutor, had learned much of the countries through which they passed, and of the history and customs of the different people. With minds naturally bright and retentive, both Harry and Laura had derived much more profit from their journeyings in foreign lands than most people do, and although they had seen so much and enjoyed so many things, they were both heartily glad to return to their own country.

It was on a bright, sunny morning in the early winter that the steamer in which Mr. Van Kuren had taken passage for himself and family, sailed up the superb harbor of New York, while the two children stood on the deck, almost screaming with delight as they recognized such familiar landmarks as the Brooklyn Bridge, Trinity steeple, the Produce Exchange, and even caught a distant glimpse of the Palisades. A tall column of smoke rising from the heart of the great city caught their eye.

"What makes that smoke?" said Harry, to his tutor who was standing beside him.

"I don't know," replied Mr. Reed, doubtfully, "But I think it must be a fire. Yes, the smoke is growing denser every moment and now we can see bits of flame in it too."

"I wonder if Bruce Decker is there, helping to put it out," exclaimed Harry, impulsively. "I tell you it must be grand to be running to the fires all the time. I wonder how Bruce is getting along, anyway. Don't you think it's funny we haven't heard a word from him?"

Laura did not reply at first but seemed to be interested only in looking intently at the familiar features of the scene about her, but when Harry repeated his question she remarked carelessly, "Oh I suppose he's too much occupied with his own affairs to bother about us. Anyway, Harry, it is not necessary for us to see him any more. He is very well in his way, but not nearly so refined and elegant in his manners as those children we used to play with in Paris. Just compare him with little Victor Dufait for example. Why Victor was the politest boy I ever saw in my life, and it would be a good thing for Bruce, and you too, to copy his manners."

"Well I'd rather copy Bruce than that little frog-eating Frenchman, any day!" cried Harry. "You think he's all right just because he bows and scrapes and grins every time he sees you coming. But if you were to play with him and the rest of those fellows, as I did, you'd soon find out that they're not half as nice as they seem. Besides, I'll bet that Bruce could lick any two of them with one hand tied behind his back."

"Well, there are better things than being able to lick other boys, even with both hands tied behind your back," rejoined Laura, "and I think that Victor is one of the nicest boys I ever met."

"Well, you can have him for all I care, but I'd like to see Bruce again, and as soon as we get ashore I'm going down to hunt him up."

"You will do nothing of the sort, Harry," interjected Mr. Reed, in a tone of quiet determination. "You may remember, perhaps, that your father has forbidden you to have anything to do with that young Decker, and I am quite sure that you at least, Laura, have not forgotten the circumstances which led to his making that rule. So I particularly caution you not to set your hearts upon renewing an acquaintance which your father does not consider a desirable one, and my advice is not to mention the matter in his presence."

The tutor's words ended all discussion of the young fireman, and very soon afterwards the children went down stairs to make their final preparations for landing. Laura had been partly in earnest in what she said about Bruce. She had made the acquaintance of several boys of foreign parentage during their stay in Paris, and had been greatly impressed with their polished manners and glib tongues. Victor Dufait, whom her brother despised, was a lad well calculated to awaken the admiration of any girl unused to superficial elegance of manners. Always handsomely dressed and neat in his appearance, he was to all outward appearances as gentlemanly and modest a lad, as one could hope to meet, but the boys who played with him knew that his politeness was, as they expressed it, "all put on," and that among lads of his own age, or younger, he could be selfish, ill-natured, and vindictive. Many a time had Harry, while playing with him and other boys of his sort, thought regretfully of the manly, good-natured, and companionable Bruce Decker, who, although of much more humble origin than the little foreigner, possessed a much truer breeding—that which comes from a good heart and kindly intentions.

From the steamer Mr. Van Kuren and his family went directly to a large and fashionable hotel on Broadway, intending to remain there until their own house could be repaired and put in thorough order. The children continued their studies under the direction of their tutor and an English governess, who had accompanied them home from London, and every afternoon went out to walk in the streets. Sometimes Harry and Mr. Reed enjoyed long strolls along the river front, where the boy never wearied of looking at the great ships and little fishing sloops, as they lay at the docks, and sometimes the two went down into the poorer portions of the town, where Mr. Reed pointed out to him the habitations of different races of people, and explained to him their curious modes of living.

Sometimes Laura accompanied them, when they walked along the principal avenues or through Central Park, but as a general thing she went out with her governess, and sometimes invited some young girl of her own age to accompany her. She was walking in this way one afternoon, talking to a richly dressed young girl, and accompanied by the prim-looking governess, when her young companion drew her attention to the fact that some one was trying to attract her attention. Laura looked up hastily and beheld Bruce Decker standing with his hat in his hand and a rosy flush on his cheeks almost in front of her. The governess was looking in wonder at the presuming young man, and the young girl beside her was beginning to laugh, for to tell the truth, Bruce presented an appearance that was not at all like that of little Victor Dufait.

"How do you do, I did not know you were back from Europe," began the boy. But to his amazement Laura, who had always treated him in a most friendly manner, simply stared him in the face, bowed to him very coldly, and then walked on with her eyes turned in another direction, and a look in her face that was anything but pleasant or cordial. And as she passed on she realized that the boy was standing stock still on the pavement behind her, amazed beyond expression at the way in which he had been treated. She knew, moreover, that what with her annoyance at her companion's sneers, and her fear lest the English governess should tell her father of the chance meeting, she had treated Bruce with a degree of harshness, which she never intended, and she would have given almost anything—at least it seemed so to her at that moment—to have been able to live the past few minutes over again.

It is no easy task to describe Bruce Decker's feelings, as he stood in the middle of the pavement on Fifth Avenue, and watched the retreating form of the young girl, whose friendship he had once prized so highly. His cheeks grew redder and redder, as he thought of the glance she had given him, and the insolence of her manner. Then he glanced down on his clothes, and his hands reddened and hardened with toil, and said to himself, "Well, I suppose I'm not stylish enough to suit her now that she's been across the water, and mixed up with all sorts of foreign people." It seemed very hard to the boy, however, that he should be despised just because he did not wear fashionable clothes, and he said to himself with some bitterness of spirit, "I suppose I could rig myself up in fine style for less than a hundred dollars, and be as good a dude as any of them."

It was with this feeling in his heart that he walked slowly away, and then—for his brain did not stop working merely because of some trifling rebuff—it occurred to him that if there was only a hundred dollars difference between him and a dude, the obstacle was not an impossible one to surmount, and that a few years of hard work would convert him into a very superior quality of dude, and would thus enable him to regain the friendship and esteem which he was positive Miss Van Kuren once entertained for him. With this cheerful view of the case he lifted his head bravely, and walked on toward the truck quarters with swift and resolute steps. He said nothing to his friend Charles Weyman in regard to his chance meeting. In fact, he did all he could to forget it himself, but he had been too deeply wounded to put all recollection of the young girl's coldness to him aside, and the memory of that chance meeting rankled in his breast for many weeks.

Chapter XXXIV.

ONE cold, dreary, windy evening, the tall, dark, bearded man left the office on the East side, where he was known as "Scar-faced Charlie," and turned his face in the direction of the fine mansion in the upper part of the city, where he was known to the servants, the tradespeople, and a few of the neighbors as "Samuel Dexter," a relative of the kindly old gentleman who owned the house. Passing through the broad gate and along the winding road, he emerged into an open space in front of the mansion, and saw to his surprise that lights were gleaming through the windows of the elder Mr. Dexter's library, a room which was seldom opened during the owner's absence.

The bearded man had been away for two or three days, and, thinking that the servants had taken advantage of his absence, to make use of an apartment into which he seldom penetrated himself, he quietly let himself in at the front door, and stepping across the hall, threw open the door of his uncle's study, intending to administer a severe rebuke to whomever he might find within.

But the angry words died away unuttered on his lips, and he started back with a look of amazement and chagrin, as Mr. Dexter, Senior, rose from an easy chair by the fire and came forward to greet him.

"Why, my dear uncle, I had no idea that you were in this country," exclaimed the new comer, as he recovered himself sufficiently to grasp the hand that was extended to him, and assume something that resembled at least a pleased expression of countenance.

"I only arrived this morning," replied the other, "and so I thought I would treat you to a pleasant surprise."

That his coming had proved a surprise, if not an altogether pleasant one, was quite apparent to the elder Mr. Dexter, who had narrowly watched his nephew's face and noted the quick change of expression that passed across it as he entered the room. Since that evening in Paris, when he had addressed to him a letter of inquiry, several things had occurred to convince the old gentleman that his kinsman was not treating him in a straightforward manner. He had replied to the letter, it is true, but in such a way as to make it apparent that he either had not troubled himself to fulfill his uncle's request, or else that he was concealing from him the information which he possessed. It was partly because of these suspicions which had taken possession of his mind, and partly because he was extremely anxious to learn more about Bruce Decker, that Mr. Dexter, Senior, determined to cut short his stay in Europe, and return at once to New York.

He had landed early that morning, and one of his first duties had been to go and see Ann Crehan, the old woman who had once been a nurse in the Van Kuren family, and who was supported now by them and by himself. The poor old creature poured into his sympathetic ear a sad tale of destitution. One of her remittances had failed to reach her, and in order to tide over a brief period, she had applied to the younger Mr. Dexter for a loan, but without success. Then, not wishing to have her true condition made known to her neighbors—for the poor are far more sensitive than the rich,—she had made up a little package of a few old pieces of silver-ware and the gold watch she cherished above all her earthly possessions, and taken them down to Eldridge Street, where "an ould blood-letting scoundrel" had loaned her a few dollars on them.

The old creature had but one anxiety now, and that was to recover her lost trinkets, and her benefactor readily promised to come the very next day—for his foreign money was not then exchanged—and bring her the funds that would enable her to do so.

On his way up-town that night, Mr. Dexter thought with bitterness and regret of the ingratitude shown him by the nephew, whom he had intended to make his heir.

"He might have spared a few dollars for old Ann Crehan, if not on my account on his own, for it was she who saved his life when he was merely a boy, and a man must be hard hearted indeed, who can forget such a service."

But despite his feelings he said nothing to his nephew about the old nurse, nor did he allude to the evasive reply which had been sent to him in Paris. On the contrary, he greeted his kinsman pleasantly, and chatted with him in his usual easy and amiable fashion until the time had come for them to separate for the night.

When the old gentleman descended to the breakfast-room the next morning, he found that his nephew had gone down-town, leaving word with the servant that he might be detained that night until a late hour.

Mr. Dexter accordingly breakfasted alone, and then called his carriage, and was driven to the elevated railroad station, where he took a train to the lower part of the city. It was twelve o'clock when, having attended to several matters of business, he betook himself to the East side tenement house, in which Ann Crehan lived. The old woman shed tears of joy when he told her he had come to redeem her little package of valuables, and, having taken from her the receipt and the address of the money-lender, he set out for Eldridge Street. Picking his way through the crowd of children who swarmed in that thickly settled part of the town, and sniffing the air, which was redolent of garbage and garlic and decaying fish, the old gentleman shook his head and sighed to think of the stern necessities which compelled the poor to live in such a quarter and in such a fashion.

"And what sort of a man must this money-lender be?" he said to himself. "I cannot see how a man, with any feelings at all in his heart, can deliberately establish himself in this quarter and devote his life to loaning money to these unfortunate creatures at rates of interest which, I doubt not, are exorbitant. Well, he will receive no exorbitant interest from me on the ten dollars he loaned to poor old Ann, for I know what the laws on usury are."

It was with this feeling in his heart that Mr. Dexter entered the shabby-looking office on Eldridge Street and, handing the receipt to the bookkeeper behind the tall desk said "Mrs. Crehan wishes to repay her loan and get back the package which she gave as security."

The bookkeeper glanced sharply at the receipt and then at the well-dressed, prosperous looking gentleman who presented it, and then went into the inner office, took the package from the safe and brought it out.

"Twelve dollars if you please" he remarked, in his brief business-like way.

"You loaned ten dollars on these articles, less than a month ago, and now you ask for twelve dollars. Do you charge twenty per cent. a month interest?" said Mr. Dexter in firm, quiet tones.

"It's twelve dollars or you don't get the stuff," retorted the accountant in a surly voice.

"You had better be very careful, sir, or you may get into trouble," rejoined Mr. Dexter speaking very sternly, and looking the other squarely in the face. "I am familiar with the usury laws of the State and they are very explicit, in matters of this sort. I advise you to hand me that package without a moment's delay and accept the sum of ten dollars and twenty-five cents, which is interest at the rate of two and one-half per cent. a month and more than you are really entitled to."

"I will do nothing of the sort!" said the old clerk raising his voice so that it reached the ears of his employer in the inner office, "and if you don't care to pay the twelve dollars you may go about your business, and I'll put the package back in the safe."

"I'll not pay any such outrageous charge!" screamed Mr. Dexter, at the very top of his voice, "and what's more if you hesitate one minute longer I'll go out and make a complaint against you to the proper authorities."

But just at this moment the door of the inner office was thrown open and the moneylender came out exclaiming "What does all this noise mean? What do you mean, sir, by coming into my place of business——"

"There's the boss now himself. You can

settle the matter with him," remarked the bookkeeper, triumphantly. But to his surprise his master neither spoke nor stirred, and he was even more surprised to see Mr. Dexter gaze fixedly at him for a moment or two and then exclaim in tones of burning contempt, "And so this is the business that you conduct, is it? Lending money to these poor people and then charging them the most outrageous rates. I suppose you thought you could take advantage of this poor old woman who saved your life at the risk of her own when you were a mere child in arms! I believed in you Samuel in spite of the warnings that I received. But now, I have done with you forever. My servants will gather your effects together and send them to you, but I forbid you to enter my premises again under any consideration whatever."

Trembling with indignation, and with his face suffused with a high color, the old gentleman picked up the package containing Ann Crehan's little treasures, laid the sum of ten dollars and twenty-five cents on the desk and departed, slamming the door behind him as he went out with such violence that every window-sash in the room rattled.

And then the tall, sinister looking man re-entered his private den, threw himself down upon a chair, and with his head bowed in an attitude of hopeless dejection muttered: "Everything has slipped from me just as I thought it was within my grasp. There is but one hope left, and that is the boy."

Chapter XXXV.

WHEN old Mr. Dexter reached his home that afternoon, he called one of his servants and ordered him to gather all of his nephew's possessions together and pack them up, to be sent away to an address which he would give them. At the same time he informed them that if his kinsman should call, he was not to be admitted to the house on any pretense whatever. Having done this, the old gentleman sat down in his library and wrote a letter to his lawyer, who was also a warm personal friend of many years' standing, and invited him to visit him the next day, in order that they might dine together, and at the same time discuss an important matter of business. This business was nothing less than the drawing up of a new will, which should deprive his renegade kinsman of any chance of profiting by his death. Never in his whole life had the warm-hearted and benevolent old gentleman been so stirred with shame and indignation as he had that day by the sudden discovery that his nephew, who

"And so this is the business you conduct, is it?"—*Page 317*.

was of his own flesh and blood, and bore his name, was making his livelihood by loaning money to poor and unfortunate people at usurious rates of interest. That a man of proper breeding and right feelings should take advantage of the necessities of the unfortunate, stirred Mr. Dexter's soul to its inmost depths.

As for the money-lender, he realized as soon as his uncle had left the office and slammed the door behind him, that in all probabilities he would never see the inheritance of which he had for so many years based his hopes. However, there was one chance left to him, and he determined to try it before abandoning all expectation forever. He must see Bruce at once, for it was possible that, through this boy, he might once more obtain influence over his uncle. Taking his hat and cane, he left his office and hurried away to the address which Bruce had given him, and it was there that he learned that the boy had found employment in the very truck-house in which his father had worked before him, and where he had often visited him.

"That was stupid enough in me," he remarked, angrily, to himself, as he strolled along toward the quarters. "I might have known that the boy's first thought after his father's death would have been to look for some sort of a job in the department. If I had only made inquiries there instead of sending that rascally newsboy up into the country, I would have found him long ago, and might have had him out of the way by this time, if I had seen the necessity for it."

As he entered the building, Charley Weyman recognized him, and went upstairs to look for the boy. "He's down there, Bruce," he said, significantly.

"Who's down there?" demanded the young lad, looking up from the book which he was reading.

"That tall chap, with the scar on his face, that you've talked about so often. And, mark my words, he means you no good. But you go down and see what he has to say, and then tell me about it before you give him any promise or agree to do anything that he asks you to."

"But perhaps he's not going to ask me anything," replied the boy. "It may be that he's come here to do me a favor."

"Don't you believe it!" retorted Weyman. "That man never goes anywhere unless it is to get something from somebody. If he offers to do you a favor, be mighty careful how you accept his offer."

Bruce went downstairs, and was very cordially greeted by the mysterious man who had caused him so many sleepless nights since the first time he had heard of him. He was surprised now to find him so agreeable and kindly in his manner, and in a few moments he forgot his good friend's caution, and found himself talking to the money-lender as freely and easily as if he had known him all his life. He told him all that he knew of his origin, and mentioned the fact that he hardly knew anything about his father's family or friends. "I came down here soon after my father's death, and the chief took me on here, got my pension for me, and has kept me here ever since. When I'm old enough I hope to join the department, and perhaps rise in it."

"What pension is that?" asked Mr. Dexter, with a sudden gleam of interest in his face.

"The department pays it to me because my father was killed in the service," replied the boy.

"Then there is no doubt about your being the son of Frank Decker, I suppose," rejoined the other, in what seemed to Bruce like a tone of disappointment.

"Of course not," he replied.

"Very well, then," continued the visitor, "so much the better for you, for you will have no trouble in establishing your identity. As I told you the other day, a legacy left to your father by some distant relatives in England has fallen to you; but in order to get it you will be obliged to go yourself to London, prove who you are, and collect the money in person. I knew your father very well indeed, and it was simply on account of my friendship for him that I have taken the trouble to look you up. I sent that little rascal of a newsboy up to the country to search for you; and if he had done what I told him to do, or if you had come to me at once, you might have obtained possession of your inheritance by this time, to say nothing of saving me a great deal of unnecessary trouble. However, I suppose you could not have helped that."

"Indeed, sir," said Bruce, very humbly, "I went up to your house two or three times but could not learn your address, and it was only when Skinny came back to the city that I found out where your office was. It was very kind of you, I'm sure, to take so much trouble for me, and when I get this money I will very gladly pay you for what you have done."

"Never mind the pay," exclaimed the money-lender, magnanimously, " I'm willing to do a great deal for the son of my old friend. Now, I suppose you have not enough money to pay for your journey to London and back, have you?"

Bruce was forced to admit that he had not sufficient funds for such an undertaking, and on learning this, the visitor went on: "Very well, I will advance you enough for your passage there and back and other necessary expenses, and you can repay me when you receive your legacy. I suppose you might get it by sending a representative there, or engaging some well-known London lawyer, but that would cost you just as much as to take the trip yourself, and besides those English people are not like Americans, and are very slow in their business methods. And, after all, a boy of your age ought to enjoy a little trip to Europe and back. It won't come in your way very often, especially when there's nearly five thousand dollars at the other end of the route."

Nearly five thousand dollars! To the young fire-lad, who had been accustomed all his life to the most rigid economy, this seemed like an enormous sum of money. And the prospect offered him so unexpectedly of obtaining it for himself, and at the same time making a journey to England almost stunned him. He was aroused from his stupor by Mr. Dexter, who asked him how soon he would be able to start.

"Any time you say," he replied, and then added hastily, "provided, of course, that Chief Trask has no objection."

At the mention of the chief's name Mr. Dexter's brow clouded, and he exclaimed in what Bruce thought rather a contemptuous and disagreeable tone, "Well, if he is a true friend of yours, he won't object to your making such a journey as I propose, and if he does object, I should think five thousand dollars would be worth more to you, than anything you've got here."

"I'll ask him," said the boy, "and let you know to-morrow. I don't think he'll put any obstacle in my way." And with this understanding the two parted, the money-lender returning to his office, and Bruce going at once to lay the matter before his friends, Charley Weyman and the chief.

Both these men declared, after careful consideration of his case, that he could not do better than accept Mr. Dexter's proposition, provided that gentleman paid him in advance enough to cover the expenses of his journey to England and back. "You don't risk anything, you see," said Weyman, "and he does, He wouldn't send you off on a wild-goose chase, if it cost him anything to do so. In fact, you've everything to gain and nothing to lose, and it's not every day in the year that a boy like you gets the chance to travel in foreign parts at somebody else's expense. Just tell him that you're ready to go, and keep a sharp lookout for anything that may turn up."

The next day, accordingly, Bruce called on Mr. Dexter at his Eldridge Street office, and made known to him the decision of his friends. "I'm ready to go whenever you think best," he added, "but, of course, as I haven't any money, you will have to give me a return ticket, and money enough for my expenses while I'm there."

"Certainly, my boy," said Mr. Dexter, with his most winning smile, and as there is a steamer that sails next Saturday for Southampton, I will engage your passage on that. Get ready to sail at three o'clock on that day, and, meantime, I advise you to keep on at your regular work and not mention to anybody what I have told you. Some one might start up and contest that will and keep you out of your rightful dues for ten years. When you get your hands on the money, you may talk about it as much as you please."

And so the young boy returned to the truck quarters, and resumed his regular work, although he could scarcely drive out of his mind the wonderful intelligence that the money-lender had conveyed to him. Meantime, Samuel Dexter seated in his Eldridge Street office, was writing a long letter to the old gentleman who had driven him from his house.

"There!" he exclaimed, as he sealed the envelope, "I think that letter will bring him to terms if nothing else will.

Chapter XXXVI.

A COLD, bitter night, with the snow falling swiftly and silently, only to be caught up by the tempestuous bursts of wind, and swept into heavy drifts of dazzling whiteness. It was snowing hard all over the great city of New York, up-town as well as down. And in the open space in front of the fine old mansion in which Mr. Dexter lived, it had gathered in great heaps, on which bright streams of light shone from the curtained window of the comfortable library. But cold and dreary and desolate as it was without, within this richly furnished room was warmth, comfort and hospitality. The master of the house was lying with a shawl thrown over his slight figure, upon a couch, which had been drawn up in front of the great open wood-fire, and about him were gathered three or four of his best friends.

Mr. Van Kuren was there, and his sister, whom the children always addressed as "Aunt Emma," and who, on account of her delicate health, seldom ventured far away from home. It must have been business of importance that brought her from the great hotel, in which they were staying, to this mansion above the Harlem river, on such a cold and tempestuous night. Another guest, a portly, grey-haired, smooth-shaven man of judicial aspect, was the lawyer, who had been summoned by Mr. Dexter, in order to draw up a new will. Neither of the Van Kuren children were present, Harry having been sent away on a short trip with his tutor, while Laura had remained at the hotel in the care of her English governess.

On a table, which had been drawn up closely to Mr. Dexter's lounge, was an open letter, which each member of the company had carefully scrutinized in turn, and with many expressions of indignation and distrust. It was the letter which the money-lender had written and sent from his office at Eldridge Street, and which had been so cruelly planned to excite and distress the kindly old gentleman, that not only his lawyer, but his intimate friends, the Van Kurens, had been hastily summoned. The doctor fearing that the shock might prove serious, if not fatal, to the venerable patient.

"I am inclined to think, on the whole,"

said Mr. Van Kuren, after he had examined the money-lender's letter for the twentieth time, "that there is not a word of truth in what he says, and that this has been written simply in the hope of bringing about a reconciliation with you. You know what my opinion of your nephew is and always has been. I told you when we talked the matter over in Paris that he was not a man to be trusted, and I was not at all surprised to learn that he had been running his little pawnshop down on the east side, and, I have no doubt, swindling every one of the unfortunates who are compelled by their necessities to deal with him. If I were you, I would throw this letter into the fire, and dismiss all thought of the matter from my mind. Don't you agree with me, sir?" he added, turning to the kindly lawyer, who had been an attentive listener to his words.

"No, Horace," said Mr. Dexter, "I am inclined to think that there is some truth in what my nephew — rascal that he is — has hinted at, and that brings me to speak of a conversation that I had with your daughter Laura at the time that we were so much together in Paris. I did not mention this before, because she regarded it as a secret, and,

I suppose, did not care to have her interest in the matter known."

Both Mr. Van Kuren and his sister smiled broadly at the thought that Laura, whom they regarded as a volatile and rather foolish young girl, should have been able to give their old friend any important or reliable information on a subject of vital importance to him, and Miss Van Kuren rejoined: "I wouldn't pay too much attention to my niece, if I were you, for she has, like most children of her age, some very romantic and silly notions."

"But I assure you," exclaimed Mr. Dexter, earnestly, "that what she told me on this occasion made quite an impression on me — an impression which has been growing stronger and stronger ever since. It was in Paris, one morning when I called at your apartment, and there was no one there but Miss Laura. She intimated that she had something of importance to say to me, and when I encouraged her to go on she told me a story about a young boy of her acquaintance who, having come up to see me on an errand, recognized, or fancied that he recognized, the house and grounds as something that he had seen in his earliest childhood.

"She gave me his address, and I actually wrote him a letter asking him to give me such information as he could about his family, but I never received any reply, for it was not long afterwards that I left Paris for Switzerland and Italy, and subsequently sailed for New York. It is just possible, therefore, that his letter may be at this very moment following me about the continent of Europe. I was rather inclined to believe that there was some grain of truth in the story, because I remembered the young lad myself quite distinctly, and he had a pleasant, bright, open face, and did not seem to be the sort of a boy who would invent a piece of pure fiction and try to palm it off as the truth."

"Who was the boy? Do you recall his name?" said Mr. Van Kuren.

"Certainly I do. He is employed in the fire department in some capacity, and his name is Bruce Decker, and there was just enough similarity between his name and mine — Dexter and Decker — to suggest ——"

"Bruce Decker!" interrupted Mr. Van Kuren savagely; well, I can tell you from my own personal experience with that young rascal, that he is quite capable of inventing any story, and of deceiving you with it as well.

And so he took Laura into his confidence, did he? Well, I have no doubt he answered your letter, and you will be very fortunate if he doesn't hunt you up, and establish some sort of a claim on you, before you realize what he's doing! Now I'll tell you my experience with that bright, honest-looking, open-faced young scamp. He got acquainted with my children, I think it was by picking Harry up in the road one afternoon, when he met with an accident, and I asked him up to dinner, so that I might see for myself, what sort of a boy he was. As you know quite well, I am very democratic in my ideas, and I don't want Harry to grow up with a notion that he's made of better clay than the boy whose coat is not quite as good as his. In fact, I have no objection to his playing with boys in humbler circumstances than himself, providing only they are decent and honest, and as this Decker lad made a very good impression on me—for there is no denying that he has a good face and decent manners—I saw no reason why he should not come to the house now and then, and I was glad to have Harry go and visit him, when he was laid up in the hospital. The first thing I knew, the young vagabond had repaid me by entering into a sly correspondence with Laura, and I discovered that she had actually been down to the hospital, to call on him, without saying a word to either her aunt or myself. As you can well imagine, I put a stop to the intimacy without a moment's delay, and as I never heard either of the children mention the boy's name again, I concluded that they had dismissed him from their thoughts, as I had from the house. Now it seems though that he has found some means of communication with Laura, and has been filling her head with this romantic story about recognizing your house and grounds. Well, I shall put a stop to that, I can tell you, and I am very sorry to think that Laura should disobey me, as she evidently has."

"My dear Horace," exclaimed Mr. Dexter, raising himself with some difficulty as he spoke, "I am very sorry I said anything that will get your daughter into trouble, and I am sure that what she learned from this lad she learned from his own lips before you forbade the intimacy. In fact, if I remember rightly, she said as much to me herself. I still have the young man's address, and to-morrow morning, or as soon as my health will allow it, I will either go to see him or send for him, and you may be sure that I will learn exactly how much truth there is in this story that he tells. Meantime, let me beg of you to say nothing to Miss Laura, for it would really break my heart to think that I had been the means of getting her into trouble."

The old gentleman seemed to be so deeply in earnest that both Mr. Van Kuren and his sister readily promised to accede to his wishes, and Mr. Van Kuren was even induced to forego the intention he had formed of going the very next morning to the quarters of the hook and ladder truck, and lodging a complaint with the chief of the battalion.

It was late when they finished their discussion, much later than they had thought, and as they arose to take their leave, a servant, coming in with an armful of wood for the fire, informed them that the snow had accumulated in such heavy drifts, as to make the roads almost impassable.

And this information was confirmed by a glance through the window at the storm which was raging without.

"You must not think of going home tonight!" exclaimed Mr. Dexter. "It will never do for you in the world, my dear Emma, to think of going out into such an awful storm as this. No, there are plenty of rooms in the house, and I will have fires built at once, so that you will be just as comfortable as you would be at that big hotel you're stopping at. Not one of you shall leave the house to-night."

"But just think of poor little Laura all alone in that great, big hotel," exclaimed Miss Van Kuren. "Suppose anything were to happen to her; why, I would never forgive myself to the last day of my life for leaving her there. And just fancy a fire breaking out in that place in the middle of the night! No, I really think that I ought to——"

"You'll stay where you are, all of you," put in the hospitable old gentleman, in a voice that was full of pleasant authority, "and as for the hotel, it's warranted strictly fire-proof. And I'm sure Laura is just as safe there as she would be if you were with her."

And so it was settled that the Van Kurens and Mr. Dexter's lawyer should remain all night. And an hour later the last light was extinguished in the old mansion, and there was no sound to be heard about it save the raging of the storm.

Chapter XXXVII.

IT is the unconsidered trifles of life which oftentimes shape human destinies.

And what trifle is there of less importance than a window-curtain swayed by the midnight breeze?

There was such a curtain swinging idly in the window of a dimly lighted room as the clocks in the tall church towers tolled the solemn hour of midnight. The wind was high now, and the snow, which had been falling for nearly six hours, was heaped upon the roofs of the tall houses, and lay in huge drifts about the streets, while the flakes which filled the keen winter air were blown so sharply in the faces of pedestrians that men found walking possible only by keeping to the middle of the street, and bending their heads down to the sharp blasts. Now and then a policeman, muffled up to his eyes, walked along, trying the doors of shops and other places of business to see that thieves were not busy during the storm.

As the night wore on, the passers-by appeared at rarer intervals, and the snow, undisturbed by man or beast, allowed itself to be whirled and twisted by the wind into fantastic shapes, that changed with every fresh gust. One o'clock sounded from many a brazen tongue, and the wind, as if it heard in the sharp, vibrant note a new signal, seemed to grow suddenly in strength and swept across the city with fiercer and louder blasts, while the snow fell in blinding masses on roof and pavement.

The same wind coming with awful fury up the broad, deserted avenue, struck with full force against the splendid hotel, and pouring through the half-open window in the dimly lighted room set the white window-curtain swaying and flapping with renewed life.

"An awful night for a fire!" muttered a belated citizen, as he mounted his doorstep and shook the snow from his clothing in his marble-tiled vestibule.

It was indeed an awful night for a fire, but the cold and weary citizen dismissed all anxiety from his mind, and sought his bed, happy in the knowledge that there were scattered about the great sleeping city fire-engines, with swift horses to draw them, and companies of vigilant, courageous men ready to hurry to the scene of disaster at a moment's warning. And very soon the belated citizen slept too, while the storm outside raged with increased fury, and the snow swept down from the heavens and was piled in great drifts beneath the shadows of the tall building.

And down in Chief Trask's quarters nearly a mile away Bruce Decker slumbered peacefully, with his turnout on the floor beside him, while the horses stamped uneasily in their stalls, and the two men on watch sat close to the stove and talked in low tones about fires that they had known on just such windy, snowy nights in years gone by. Outside the truck-house the wind howled dismally, and the snow swept through the street in pitiless, blinding gusts, while up-town the same blasts paused for a moment in their northerly flight to play with the white window-curtain that was swinging and flapping now with increased violence in the half-lighted chamber.

And throughout the storm Bruce slept as calmly as a child, knowing nothing of all that that window-curtain meant for him. A gust fiercer than the others tore the light band which held the curtain to the wall and sent it fluttering against the gas jet. It blazed up and caught the woodwork about the window and then another gust of wind, pausing in its swift flight to the far north, scattered the blazing particles about the room, and fanned the flames that were eating their way through the handsome woodwork. Outside, beneath the window where the curtain had flapped for a moment before, the snow lay in huge untrodden drifts. There was no one there to note the blaze which had started in the room on the fifth floor, nor was there any chance watcher in the silent houses over the way to give the alarm.

It was twenty minutes after one when the idle wind blew the curtain against the flame, and at precisely twenty-five minutes of two a servant rushed, bareheaded, into the street, and, breaking for himself a path through the heavy drifts of snow, made straight for a lamp-post with red glass in its lamp that stood two blocks away. There was a red box on this lamp-post, and, although his fingers were numb with cold, the servant had it open in a jiffy, and in another second had pulled down the hook which he found inside. Before he had removed his hand from the box the number of the station had been received at headquarters and the night operator had sent the alarm to the companies in the immediate vicinity of the fire. A few seconds later half a dozen truck and engine companies, warned by the electric current, had started from their quarters and were on their way through the fierce, pelting storm. The men were buttoning their coats and pulling their fire-helmets well down over their heads as they were borne on truck and engine through the silent streets. There was no time for ceremony or roll-call in the houses into which the electricity had come with its dread warning. Not one of those men against whose stern, set faces the wind blew the keen flakes of snow, knew what awaited him at the end of this midnight journey. They were actuated by but one purpose, and that was to be at the fire as soon as possible.

And as the firemen bore down in swift flight from the four points of the compass upon the doomed structure, servants went hurrying through the corridors, knocking on every door and arousing the sleeping guests with shrill cries of "Fire!" Men, women, and children were emerging from their rooms, some calm and cool, others stricken with an awful terror, some in their night-clothes, and others partly dressed, and all hurrying as fast as they could to the staircase or elevator.

And then a cry went up in every corridor, "The elevator's afire! Make for the staircase!"

It was indeed true. The elevator shaft, acting as a draft like the tall chimney of a manufactory, had drawn the flames toward itself with resistless force, and the fire was now roaring and raving up the square shaft, burning the woodwork and spreading destruction from floor to floor.

A stranger, seeing the awful conflagration that had broken out so suddenly on that night of storm and snow, would have said, without hesitation, that the city was doomed to a repetition of that hurricane of smoke and flames that swept through Chicago years ago, and left of that fair city nothing but a waste of smoking ashes. The most destructive of all elements had begun its deadly work, and who could say what limit there would be to the destruction of life and property which would result?

But, happily for the sleeping city, there was arrayed that night against the devouring flames, the Fire Department of New York—the bravest and brainiest of men, armed with the finest appliances that modern science could produce—and it was with a knowledge

"The horses bounded to their places."—*Page 343.*

of that fact and with a confidence in the courage, skill and fidelity of this branch of the municipal government, that men and women throughout the snow-covered town slept on peacefully throughout the storm.

And the electricity flashing along the wire from the headquarters up-town entered the silent truck house ruled by Chief Trask, and with one stroke of the gong transformed it into a scene of activity. The men who were on watch on the ground floor, sprang from their seats by the stove, and the horses, released by the electric current, bounded to their places, three in front of the heavy truck, and one between the shafts of the chief's red wagon.

And the same alarm which rang out in the lower floor, sounded also in the room above, where the men lay sleeping. Bruce heard it just as he was dreaming of the old days in the village beside Lake Ontario, and he sprang to the floor, and struggled into his turnout, before he fairly realized that he was in New York, and not in the country. But, quick as he was, he was not a second ahead of the other men, and as he slid down one of the shining poles, he found that fully half the company had got down before him. By this time the horses were all in their places, and the men had just finished hitching. The alarm was still ringing on the gong, and although Charley Weyman leaped to his place in the driver's seat, the company did not start. It was a first alarm, but not one on which they were due. For a few moments they waited, while the horses tugged and strained at their bits, and stamped on the wooden floor in their eagerness to be off. Then the second alarm came, and Tom Brophy, who was at the wheel, drew on a pair of heavy woolen mittens, while the men pulled their thick caps down over their heads, and Weyman exclaimed, "Look out, fellows, we'll get a third for that, sure!"

Bruce had watched these preparations with considerable excitement, and at the suggestion of one of the men, had pulled on a heavy skull-cap, and buttoned his thick overcoat close up to his neck. He was trembling violently, but whether it was from the cold or excitement he did not know. He had never been out on a third alarm before, and the thought that the very next minute might send him out into the biting storm on an errand such as the one that had cost his father his life, sent the blood tingling through his veins.

"Jump in, Bruce!"

It was Chief Trask who said this. And as the boy made answer he continued in his sharp soldierly voice, "If we get a third alarm I want you to come with me in the wagon."

The words were scarcely out of his mouth when the brass gong sounded for a third time, and almost instantly the doors were thrown back with a roar and rumble, there was a rattle of the ropes which supported the harness, as Weyman pulled his reins with a sharp and sudden jerk, and Bruce, who by this time was seated in the chief's wagon with his superior officer beside him, felt the horse bounding forward, and the next moment was out in the blinding storm.

Strange to say he had kept his wits about him and knew in what part of the town the alarm-box from which the signal had come was situated. As they passed over the threshold, Chief Trask turned the horse sharply to the left, and then without a word, placed the reins in the boy's hands, stooped down and drew his helmet from under the seat of the wagon, and put it on, and then buttoned his jacket tightly about his neck and peered forward through the falling snow trying to catch a glimpse of the distant fire.

"And now my chance has come," said Bruce Decker to himself, for what with the cold air in his face and the necessity for careful driving, his excitement had vanished, and he felt as cool as one of the snowflakes that settled on his cheek. "I'm going to a big fire now, and I'm going to make a record if it costs me a leg."

And he drove on through the snow with Chief Trask sitting in silence by his side, and the hook and ladder company thundering along close behind them.

"Turn here?" he said to his superior as they drew near a broad thoroughfare leading up-town.

"Yes, and hurry up too," was the reply, and as he pulled the horse's head around at the intersection of the two streets, he saw several blocks ahead of him a brilliant, ruddy glare on the white snow that showed where the conflagration was. He knew at once that it was a big fire, and just then Charley Weyman, who had been rapidly gaining on him, turned his horses to the left and attempted to go by him. This was something the boy had not been looking for; he well knew that bad as it was to be beaten in the race to a fire by a rival company, it would be still worse to be passed on the way by his own truck which he was supposed to lead. Charley was driving the three strong horses that belonged to the apparatus, and Bruce held the reins over a sturdy black that had been recently added to the quarters for the chief's special use. In an instant he had grasped the whip from its socket, and brought it down on the broad, snowflaked back in front of him, causing the animal to bound forward at a slightly increased gait, but not fast enough to prevent Charles Weyman's team from creeping slowly up to him. Again he swung his whip, and they raced along, the boy driving with so much vigor and skill that he soon forged ahead, and took a lead of fully twenty yards, which he maintained until they reached the scene of the disaster. Then he pulled up. The chief leaped to the ground, and just then the truck thundered along with the captain standing on the turntable close to the driver into whose ears he had been shouting his orders.

Chapter XXXVI.

AS the chief leaped from his wagon, Bruce realized for the first time the extent of the conflagration which they had been called upon to subdue. From the upper windows of the hotel streams of smoke were issuing, while in others he could see the half-clad forms of men and women who were looking out and shouting to those in the street below for assistance.

The sidewalk in front of the main entrance was already thronged with people, many of whom were only partly dressed, and had evidently been aroused from their beds by the alarm of fire. One or two of them carried bundles in their hand, and there were some who had dragged their trunks down the stairs and out into the roadway, and were now sitting on them, regarding, in a bewildered fashion, the progress of the fire.

And now the people in the windows above began to throw satchels and other light articles out into the street, and one or two of them fell near enough to the spot where

Bruce was sitting in his wagon to make it apparent to him that he had better move away. His horse was panting and sweating from the exertion of his run, and so the boy threw a heavy blanket over him, and then hitched him to a lamp-post a block away. Then he returned to the truck, and stood for a moment watching the streams of water which the firemen were turning on the hotel.

Chief Trask, who, at the moment of his arrival had reported to the deputy in charge of the fire, now appeared and ordered his men to come up at once and open the roof; and, in obedience to this command, some of them seized axes and others hooks and endeavored to force an entrance into the building next door to the hotel. But the door resisted their attempts, and then Chief Trask briefly ordered them to get the ram.

The ram, a heavy-headed iron shaft, with handles projecting on either side, was brought from the truck, and in the hands of three or four of the strongest men of the company, soon proved formidable enough to demolish the heavy front door, and afford the firemen means of access to the building. In they went, with roof-ropes and hoisting tools, Bruce following with his iron hook in his hand; and as soon as they had broken their way to the staircase, they went up on a swift run and were not long in reaching the skylight. In an instant they had unfastened the scuttle and were out on the roof in the midst of the wind and the snow. Beside them towered the wall of the hotel, fully twenty-five feet above the roof, on which they were standing.

"Cap, get up a thirty-five-foot ladder for that roof, as quick as you can!" commanded the chief; and in a moment a long rope was uncoiled, and one end thrown over the edge of the building to the men below. To these the chief shouted his directions, lying at full length on the snow-covered roof, and bending his head down over the cornice in a difficult attempt to make himself heard. Then a thirty-five-foot ladder, with the end of the rope tied around its sides and under its middle rounds was reared against the wall, and with a strong pull the chief and his followers pulled it up until it was within their reach.

Once on the roof, the ladder was speedily raised, and placed as securely as it was possible to place it against the wall of the burning hotel. Then, with the chief leading and

Bruce bringing up the rear, the men made the ascent, and stood at last on the parapet of the building, from which they descended to the tin roof. The smoke was rising about them now in dense clouds, and the chief knowing that the hotel itself must be filled with it, ordered his men to begin at once the task of breaking skylights and ventilators and cutting a hole in the tin roof to serve as a vent.

To this task the firemen bent themselves with characteristic energy, cutting a big square hole with their axes, and then turning back the tin with their hooks. This done, it was an easy matter to break through the boards and plaster that formed the ceiling, and thus give a vent to the smoke and flames. In the meantime other axemen had demolished one of the scuttles, so that dense clouds, enlivened here and there by brilliant tongues of fire, were pouring out through the two huge openings.

As the men stood resting after their labors, and waiting for further orders from the chief, Bruce crept along to the edge of the roof, and leaning over it looked down into the street below. He could see that fully a dozen fire-engines were at work now. He could hear the noise they made, and it sounded like the distant strokes of so many pile-drivers. The police had arrived by this time, and driven the crowd back from in front of the hotel, leaving none there but the firemen and some of the escaping guests. The snow which lay so white and pure on the roofs and in the other streets that were within his range of vision, was trampled into a black slush, while the heat of the flames had already melted some of the drifts that lay close at hand.

A fire-escape, connecting the different stories of the burning building, attracted his attention, and it seemed to him to be crowded with frightened people who were hurrying down it as fast as they could, some carrying bags or bundles, while others who had not even taken time to dress, were in their night clothes, and apparently perfectly oblivious of the awful storm of wind and snow that raged about them. And as he noted all these things he saw coming down the broad avenue a fire-engine driven at the top of the horses' speed and belching out a column of black smoke from its funnel, while the red-hot cinders, falling from the ash-pan, sizzled and then went out in little breaths of steam in the snow that lay thick on the streets. And now a sudden shout arose from the men and women on the fire-escape, and was echoed by those in the street underneath. The boy looked down, startled by the loud cries, and saw the flames bursting out of the building at the sixth story, completely enveloping the frail iron stairway on which the hapless guests were going down, and cutting off the escape of those who still lingered on the upper floors. He saw at once the danger in which these people were, and realized that in their half-crazed condition they were liable to throw themselves to the ground.

"Chief!" he cried, running over to the scuttle where that officer stood, "there are a lot of people on the fire-escape and the flames are coming out right under them. Can't we save them?" In an instant Chief Trask had run to the edge of the roof, and thrown himself at full length on the snow covered surface so that he could look down as the boy had a few moments before.

"Hold on there!" he yelled to those who found themselves cut off, and who seemed ready to take the most desperate chances to save their lives. "Don't jump! Stay right where you are and we'll save you in a couple of minutes."

His words and the authoritative way in which they were uttered made an instant impression on the frightened men and women to whom they were addressed, and when these looked up above them and saw the helmet of a fireman extended beyond the cornice, they felt assured that succor was at hand, and despite their awful position of peril they gave vent to a feeble cheer.

"Go back into the hotel!" screamed Chief Trask at the top of his lungs, for the wind was blowing so fiercely that it was with great difficulty he could make himself heard.

"We can't go back! We were driven out by the smoke!" yelled a man in stentorian tones.

"I tell you to go back at once and I'll come down with my men and take you out of the building," rejoined the fireman in stern, commanding tones, which left the frightened guests no alternative but to obey. Accordingly they climbed in at the windows from which they had escaped, and found that the rooms were no longer filled with smoke, as they had been before, because, although they did not know it, the open skylight and holes made in the roof by the firemen had drawn most of the smoke out of the building, and made it possible for people to move about in the upper stories without fear of suffocation.

Having seen that his orders were obeyed, Chief Trask lifted a scuttle which had not previously been touched by the firemen, and finding that very little smoke came up through the open hatchway, and also that the volumes that were pouring through the other apertures were not nearly as dense or as black as they were before, he summoned his men, and, leading the way himself, bade them follow into the interior of the hotel. Bruce went with him, leaving the scuttle open behind him.

Meantime the firemen outside the building had not been idle. There were twelve fire-engines on the ground, four hook and ladder companies and a water-tower, and of these four engine companies had been ordered to enter the hotel by the main entrance, while four more had gone around to the side and rear entrances, and the others were at work in the streets throwing water against the burning wall and also upon the roofs of the buildings adjoining. As for the hook and ladder companies, some of them were in the building helping to tear down partitions and ceilings, while others had put up their scaling ladders and were going from window to window in order to save any people who might be imprisoned in the rooms. Others had ascended to the roofs of the neighboring houses, and were lending efficient aid to the firemen by helping to haul the long lengths of hose up from the street.

At this critical moment, and when the fire seemed to be making steady headway in spite of the desperate and diligent efforts of those who were fighting it, the sharp clang of a gong was heard on the street, and immediately the crowd which had gathered, despite the awful storm that was raging, parted in the middle. The policemen on guard saluted, and a wagon, drawn by a panting and sweating horse, dashed through the fire-lines and drew up suddenly at the curb-stone. The tall, grizzled, and soldierly looking man who alighted was evidently a person of importance, for in an instant the deputy chief in command of operations appeared before him and saluted him in military style.

The new comer was tall and well built. He wore a thick fireman's overcoat and a helmet. His face was grave and stern, and smooth shaved, save for a grey moustache.

"What have you sent out?" he demanded curtly of his deputy, as with a quick glance of his practiced eye he took in all the details of the scene in which he found himself.

"Third, sir."

Once more the chief of the fire department surveyed the burning building before him. Then, without a word, he turned on his heel and walked rapidly to the corner of the street, where he could have a better view of the fire and of its exposure on all sides. He was back again in less than a minute, and ordered his subordinate to send out a special call for two engines and a truck company, in order to locate more companies on the north side of the fire. Then he ordered the immediate erection of a water-tower on the eastern side, and stood silently regarding the men, as they placed it in position.

About this time the fuel-wagons sent out by the companies which had arrived on the first and second alarms, began to come in loaded with cans of coal, and with small boys sitting on them ready to lift them to the ground and make themselves as useful as possible, simply for the sake of being inside the fire-lines and imagining themselves to be firemen. There is no fire in New York, no matter at what time of the day or the night, that does not attract its swarm of boys, who are only too anxious to load and unload the fuel-cans, in order to get into the thick of the excitement.

Chapter XXXIX.

MEANWHILE our young hero—for hero he was truly showing himself to be—was following the chief into the interior of the dark and burning hotel. Groping their way along through the corridors, sometimes finding the smoke so thick and black that they were obliged to crawl along on their hands and knees, they made the best of their way to the place where the fire was raging. As they crawled along, they encountered a number of frightened guests, some of whom had come in from the fire-escape at the chief's command, while nearly all of them were too much terrified to fairly understand what they were about. One lady, who had thrown a black silk dress over her night-clothes, carried a barking poodle-dog under her arm, while another clung tenaciously to a bird-cage, in which was a green parrot, although, as it afterwards transpired, she had left her gold watch and casket of jewels under the pillow of her bed. Some of these people cried, while others were silent, and one man, on whom they stumbled, was lying at full length in an open doorway, unconscious from the effects of the smoke.

At the chief's command two firemen carried him at once to the window, where the fresh air soon revived him, and he was lowered by means of a life-line, tied under his arms, to the ground below. By the same method several other guests were saved, though others, including the two woman already named, positively refused to go down in such an undignified manner.

While this was going on, Bruce, carrying his hook, and still following the members of his company, descended to the floor below, and then, hearing voices below him, went down one more flight of stairs, and encountered Captain Murphy's men, who had made their way up from the lower entrance. At the chief's command, Bruce and two other men went into one of the bedrooms, threw open a window, and, lowering a long line, called upon the men below to attach their hose to it, so that they might draw it up.

Chief Trask had often told Bruce that in the work of fighting a fire the most important thing is to discover the location of the flames, and not only subdue them but prevent them from spreading to other parts of the building. In order to do this, it is necessary to cover all exposed parts, and to saturate with water everything of an inflammable nature that lies near the seat of the conflagration. In this particular case, the snow which covered the roofs of the adjacent buildings prevented anything like danger from flying sparks and cinders, but had the fire taken place during dry, summer weather, one of the first duties of the firemen would have been to throw water on every roof and wall that lay within possible reach of the longest tongue of flame.

Working in the interior of the hotel, the firemen, under Chief Trask's direction, bent their energies toward arresting the possible spread of the flames, which had already gained such headway by means of the elevator shaft that it seemed to an inexperienced young fire-lad, like Bruce, an almost hopeless task to attack them. But with the aid of the hose which had been hauled up through the window, all the partitions, floors and ceilings were speedily saturated with water, while the men tore down with their hooks a number of frame partitions, in order to prevent the spread of fire through the lath and plaster.

"Bruce!" cried Brophy, coming up suddenly to where the boy was standing, "the chief says for you to go right down and tell Captain Murphy's engineer to give us more pressure."

"All right," replied the boy promptly, and pulling his helmet well down and his coat collar up about his mouth, he started down the winding marble staircase that led to the lower floor. It was a perilous journey, for the smoke filled the air, and through the darkness he could see shooting tongues of flame and showers of sparks, showing that the fire was eating its way into the woodwork and consuming both walls and floors with terrible persistence. But Bruce was not the boy to be daunted by heavy smoke and crumbling floors, and besides he felt that he was a full-fledged fireman now, for had he not received his baptism of fire a year ago? So he stumbled down the stairs, clinging to the balustrade, and soon the atmosphere grew clearer and the light stronger, and then he stepped on a marble floor covered with at least six inches of water, and realized that he was standing in what had been but a few hours before the gorgeous entrance to one of the most sumptuous hotels in New York. Clerks and servants were running to and fro, carrying out different articles of value, and Bruce noticed three or four red-helmeted insurance patrolmen, who were going about placing covers over some of the more costly fittings, in order to protect them from the deluge of water from above.

Through the entrance the boy rushed out into the street, and looked about him for Captain Murphy's engine. The snow was still falling, but it was so trampled under foot that the street looked like one huge puddle of black, filthy water, filled with enormous twisting and writhing serpents. These were the lengths of hose which were scattered about in all directions.

The reporters had arrived by this time and passed the fire-lines, and he could see them darting about, with their note-books in their hands, jotting down bits of description and facts of interest regarding the fire, while one or two of them were sending messengers down-town, in order that their city editors might issue extra editions of the newspapers if they deemed the fire of sufficient importance.

Bruce soon found the company he was in search of. The engineer, on receipt of the chief's orders, proceeded to lock his relief-valve, and give his fire an extra shake with his "slice-bar," as he called the long iron poker used for stirring up the coal. Then he opened his throttle a little wider, at the same time placing his foot upon the hose leading to the roof, and giving it a sharp, vicious stamp, to find out if the increased pressure had made it any harder.

Bruce stood beside him, an observant watcher of everything he did; and then remarked, as he turned his eyes to the burning building, "It looks as if it were getting away from them."

"Well, it does look somewhat that way," rejoined the engineer, unconcernedly, as he threw more coal into his engine. He was an old fireman, and had seen too many big blazes to be particularly stirred up by such an one as this.

Bruce turned away, wishing that he could go to a fire in the same calm, professional mood, and bent his steps toward the building adjoining the hotel, through which Chief Trask's company had first ascended to the roof. He had found the passage by the hotel staircase too perilous and difficult to be attempted again, particularly as the flames seemed to be making such fearful headway, despite the utmost exertions of the men who were fighting them. But as he was crossing the street he turned his eyes upward, and caught a glimpse of Chief Trask climbing down the long ladder that stood against the side of the hotel. Bruce knew at once what it meant. His company had been ordered to abandon their position and return to the street. And so he determined to wait until they came down. He was standing on the corner, still undecided as to what course he should pursue, when he heard a faint scream, and on looking up he saw in one of the windows on the fifth floor, a slender, white-robed figure. Some one, a young girl it seemed to him, was in imminent danger, and it looked as if she were preparing to climb over the sill and throw herself into the street.

"Don't jump! stay where you are!" yelled the young fire-lad at the top of his lungs.

The young girl in the window heard him, for she paused and shouted some unintelligible answer, to which he replied—for a sudden idea had taken possession of him—"Stay where you are! I'll be with you in a minute!"

There was no time for hesitation or reflection now. Trained as he was to the immense value which the smallest fraction of time possesses in the eyes of a true fireman, he realized, for the first time in his life, how precious even a single second may be. A hook and ladder truck stood within ten feet of him, and it seemed to the boy that within one of these precious seconds he had reached it, and seized one of the light scaling ladders that hung at its side. With this in his hands he rushed toward the hotel, attached the hooks at the ladder's end to the sill of a window directly under that in which the white-robed young girl was standing, and had just placed his foot on the lower rung, when some one seized him by the shoulder.

"Hold on there! You've forgotten something!"

It was one of the reporters, and as Bruce heard him he realized that he had forgotten to put on a belt and provide himself with a life-line. There was the belt with its big iron hook attached to the ladder, and while he was fastening it about his waist, the reporter ran to the truck, and came flying back with a life-line coiled about his arm.

"Up with you!" he cried, as he handed it to the boy, and added, as Bruce, with his eyes fixed on the window above him, and the life-line held firmly in his hand, began the ascent, "and may God bless you!"

Then the reporter jumped back to the other side of the street, and, lifting his voice above the noises that filled the air, cried, "Stay where you are! he's coming right up to you!" But even as he spoke the room in which the young girl stood was lit up with a flash of light, and then the smoke came in through the blazing door, and began to pour out of the window above her head in a dark, heavy stream.

On went Bruce to the top of his ladder. Then, throwing his leg over the window-sill, he hastily pulled up his frail wooden stairway, and by the exercise of all the coolness, skill and rapidity at his command, fastened the hooks over the window-sill of the room to which he was climbing. Then on and up again through the smoke, which was gaining strength every moment, and was whirled into his face by the pitiless storm of wind. The heat was terrible, and the side of the building so hot that it blistered his hands to touch it. But he gave no thought to smoke, flame or heat. His only hope was to reach that window above him before it was too late. And to the young girl who stood there in peril of her life, every second seemed a full hour, until at last the helmeted head rose above the level of the sill.

Bruce had all his wits about him now, for he knew that he stood in need of every particle of nerve and courage and decision that he possessed, and that a single slip or false step on his part meant death, perhaps, to them both—to him as well as to the white-robed, slender girl, who was leaning, half fainting, against the window-frame, her fair hair falling in a wild tangle down her shoulders, her hands clasped, and her lips moving as if in prayer.

With a quick bound the young fireman scrambled over the window-sill and into the room. Then taking his life-line, he began to uncoil it, and, stretching out his arms to the young girl, said, in a calm, steady voice: "Don't be frightened!" It was then that their eyes met for the first time, and Bruce Decker found himself standing face to face with Laura Van Kuren, while the storm of wind and snow was raging outside and the smoke and flame were creeping up behind him.

His clothing was torn and soiled, his face and hands grimy with sweat and smoke. The snow and the ashes had fallen upon him unheeded, and the flames had singed and burnt his clothing in a dozen places. But never did the bravest, handsomest soldier on parade seem to any one as heroic and courageous and manly as did Bruce to the young girl who almost fell into his outstretched arms, while she murmured, "Oh! Bruce, it is you! I thought you would never come."

But the boy uttered never a word, and a sharp pang pierced Laura's heart as she remembered their last meeting in the street, when she had been ashamed of him. She was not ashamed of him now, and as she rested in his strong arms, with her cheek against his wet coat, she thanked Heaven that it was he, and not the little French boy, Victor, who had come to save her. And now Bruce had slipped the life-line around her, and tied it firmly under her arms, and, having taken a turn or two of the slack about his belt-hook, disengaged her clinging arms from about his neck, and prepared to lower her to the sidewalk.

"Aren't you coming too, Bruce?" she asked, faintly.

"Afterwards," was all he said. And then she was swung off into mid-aid, and felt her-

self going down through the smoke and the flames and the storm, and she knew no more until she found herself in the arms of a brawny fireman on the pavement.

Her first thought was of the boy who had saved her. But when she looked up at the window from which she had come she could see nothing, for the flames had burst out from beneath it, cutting off every hope of escape.

"Has he come down? Is he safe?" she asked. But there was no reply, for those that stood about her looked at one another with expressive glances and shook their heads, and then turned their eyes toward the awful flames which were sweeping with resistless force up the side of the building.

Laura closed her eyes and covered her face with her hands, and just then a mighty shout rent the air. The boy had appeared at another window — he had made his line fast to the sill and thrown the loose end down into the street! And now he was climbing out of the window, and a great silence fell upon the crowd as, with one look at what lay before him, he deftly twisted the frail rope about his belt-hook, and, with a firm grasp on the line below, plunged into the whirlwind of flame and smoke beneath him.

"The boy's all right, miss; he's just come down from another window. He's standing there on the pavement," were the words that fell upon the young girl's ear. She heard them, but made no response — her overtaxed strength had given way.

And now it became apparent to others beside Captain Murphy's engineer that the great hotel was doomed. The chief of the department, who had been a silent and apparently unmoved spectator of all that has just been described, realized it, too, and uttered the simple command: "Back out!" The order was given none too soon, and as the long lines of hose were withdrawn, the firemen broke them up into convenient lengths and attached them to the four-inch stand-pipe on the deck of the water-tower, while others made preparations to take positions on the adjacent buildings, in order to operate the siamese streams. Then the men swarmed up and through the houses near by bearing hose-hoists and roof-ropes, and in a few minutes they were hauling long lines of pipe up over the eaves of the houses, and fastening them securely, by means of the roof-ropes, to chimney and scuttle. Two, three, and four way siamese connections were quickly placed in position, and connected with the huge brass stand-pipe with incredible rapidity, and from these great volumes of water were poured against and into the doomed building and upon the roofs of the houses next to it.

And now an awful crash, and a huge pyramid of smoke, sparks and flames told the watchers that the roof had fallen in. Soon afterwards the front wall fell, and then the two side walls went down, leaving a huge mass of cinders, bricks and ashes, where the great hotel had stood when the sun went down.

The new day was just beginning to dawn, when the welcome order came from Chief Trask to the various companies which had been operating under him, "Report to the Chief," and each captain went at once to where the officer stood, surveying the scene of desolation, and repeating the chief's order.

"Take up," was the silent man's rejoinder, and the wearied men gathered up their hose, placed it in well-ordered layers in the hose wagon, unblanketed the horses, and, carefully picking their way among the lengths of hose which were still lying on the ground, returned to their quarters.

Meantime, under orders of the chief of the department, three or four spare battalion engines moved into advantageous positions, and to these were attached the lines of the companies at work. A detail of engineers and men was quickly made, and then the brief order to "take up" sent the others away from the scene of the fire. As the day broke, men and women going to their daily toil stopped to look at the smoking heap, on which two or three streams were falling from the spare engines. By noon the snow had fallen upon the ruins, and but a single hydrant line remained in operation.

Chapter XXXX.

Mr. Van Kuren arose at a very early hour the next morning and came down stairs to the dining room with the intention of taking a hasty breakfast and departing at once for his office. But despite the unseasonable hour his host was there before him, looking so pale and worn that his guest inquired anxiously if he had passed a sleepless night or if anything unusual had happened to disturb him.

"My dear Horace," said Mr. Dexter with great earnestness, "I hardly slept at all last night, for not only have I been completely upset by these matters which we have already discussed, but this morning about two o'clock I noticed a bright glare on the southern skies which soon assumed such proportions that I knew there must be a very large fire somewhere in the heart of the city. As a general thing fires do not cause me any uneasiness but what could I think of last night except that hotel in which your daughter was sleeping, with none of her own flesh and blood near her? For fully three hours I sat watching the light of that conflagration, which must have been a very large one, and I could think of nothing but Laura. I got up early hoping to find something in the newspapers that might rid my mind of worry; but the servant tells me that the snow has fallen so as to make the streets almost impassable, and the boy who supplies us has not yet appeared. If he does not come very soon I shall send my own man to the nearest news-stand for I assure you that I have been very much worried."

"My dear old friend," said Mr. Van Kuren gently as he placed his hand affectionately on the old gentleman's shoulder, "you really must not allow such trivial things to worry you and keep you awake. I went to that hotel principally because I was assured that it was thoroughly fire-proof and you may depend upon it that that fire last night was miles further down town. However, you may rest assured that if anything alarming has happened, I will send you word at once. But whatever you do," he added, "be sure you say nothing of this to my sister. The shock or the anxiety might prove a very serious matter to her in her present condition of health."

"I have another request to make of you, Horace," continued Mr. Dexter speaking with even more earnestness than before, "and that is that you go to the engine house in which that young man Decker is employed and learn from his own lips all that you can in regard to his family. If you find that what Sam hinted at is true, bring him here without a moment's delay. I am a very old man, Horace, but this is a matter which must be settled at once for I can bear the suspense no longer."

Mr. Van Kuren readily gave the required promise, and having eaten a light breakfast he entered Mr. Dexter's carriage and was driven off in the direction of the Elevated railroad. Purchasing a copy of a morning paper, he entered the car and settled himself in a corner to read the news. As he unfolded the damp sheet his eye fell upon a headline in heavy black type which told him at once that something exciting had occured. The next moment the color left his cheeks and his hands began to shake so that he could scarcely read. The great hotel in which he and his family had lodged had been destroyed by fire and a number of the guests were known to have perished. There was no list of the missing or of the saved, and he realized that it would be impossible for him to learn any further details without going himself to the scene of the disaster. He read the short description of the fire through, and then the paper slipped from his hands and fell unheeded to the floor of the car, while he sat literally stunned by what he had just learned aud apparently unable to collect his thoughts or make up his mind what to do.

Other people about him, who had noticed the bright glare on the sky the night before were talking about the fire, and discussing the probable number of the missing. It was this that roused him from his stupor and he sat bolt upright in his seat, picked up the paper again and once more carefully perused the account of the conflagration. He was still fully two miles from 42d St., the station nearest to the great heap of cinders, bricks and ashes in which perhaps his own daughter was buried.

The train seemed to crawl at a snail's pace and it was in vain that he tried to divert his attention, from what he had just learned by reading the other portions of the newspaper. Again and again his eyes would turn to the awful black headline on the front page, and finally he threw the sheet to the floor in despair, folded his arms across his breast and endeavored to think of something else. But there was one figure which he could not blot out of his mind.

It was that of his daughter standing by an open window with clothes and hair ablaze and screaming for some one to save her.

At last the train stopped at 42d St., and the distracted father flew down the steps to the sidewalk, called to a hack-man who was standing near and bade him drive him at full speed to the scene of the fire. The snow was still falling when he reached his destination and a large crowd had gathered to view the smoking ruin. A number of firemen were there and there were still two or three streams in operation. Three well dressed gentlemen were standing on the corner of the street watching everything attentively, and as Mr. Van Kuren alighted from his cab he recognized one of the group as Mr. Peter Dewsnap, an old acquaintance of his.

"Big fire this" exclaimed Mr. Dewsnap as the other approached him, "and I'm afraid there are a good many bodies down there under that heap of bricks and mortar. There, they're bringing a body out now," he went on eagerly, never thinking what his words meant to the man whose only daughter had been a guest in the hotel the night before. The crowd parted to make way for four men who bore between them a rough stretcher on which lay a shapeless object covered with a blanket.

"What's that?" demanded Mr. Van Kuren, hoarsely, as he placed a detaining hand on the arm of one of the bearers, "a man, or a woman, or a child?"

"Man, sir," was the answer.

"Thank God for that!" exclaimed the father so fervently that Mr. Dewsnap glanced at him with a sudden apprehension and exclaimed, "Did you have any friends or relatives in the hotel?"

"My daughter slept here last night, and I do not know whether she is alive or not this morning," was the reply uttered in tones of heart-rending despair that had an instant effect upon Mr. Dewsnap's kindly and sympathetic heart.

"What!" he exclaimed, "your daughter in that hotel and you do not know whether she was saved or not? Was she a young lady or merely a child?"

"Between the two," replied Mr. Van Kuren sadly.

"I wonder if it could have been that young girl who was saved by that young friend of yours," exclaimed one of Mr. Dewsnap's companions, none other than the honorable Mr. Rupert Doubter who has already been introduced to our readers, and was now an enthusiastic admirer of and believer in the New York Fire Department.

"Very likely, indeed," cried Mr. Dewsnap excitedly. "She seemed to be a young girl of about fifteen, and she was lowered from a window in the fifth floor by a young friend of mine and very proud we all are of him, too. The child had been left in the care of her governess, who slept in an adjoining room and was found lying on the floor unconscious from the effect of the smoke. She had probably started to go into the next room and awaken her young charge and had fallen down, overcome by the dense clouds of smoke. Both she and the young girl were taken to that hotel on the next block and are probably there now, but really, if you could have seen the way that boy—" but Mr. Van Kuren was already on his way to the hotel and out of hearing.

Ten minutes later he was standing in one of the rooms in the hotel with his child clasped tightly in his arms and she was saying to him: "Oh, papa, if it had not been for him I would have been burnt up. I had just given myself up for lost when he came up the ladder, put a rope around my waist and let me down. I cannot bear to think of the way we have treated him and especially the way I treated him when

I met him in the street the other day." And Laura hid her head in her father's breast and sobbed aloud.

"Treated whom? My darling," demanded Mr. Van Kuren. "Who was it that saved you?"

"Why, Bruce Decker, papa. Who else could it be?"

Chapter XXXXI.

DOWN at Chief Trask's quarters Bruce was quietly resting after the excitement and fatigue of the night before, when to his surprise he saw Mr. Van Kuren cross the threshold, and he was even more surprised when that gentleman seized him by the hand and with an emotion that showed itself in his voice as well as his face, thanked him for his heroism in saving Laura from the flames. The young boy's cheeks burned as he listened to the older man's expressions of praise and gratitude. He had been so accustomed to hearing of and sometimes seeing deeds of gallantry that it had not occurred to him that he had done anything remarkable. That it had been his good fortune to render a great service to Laura Van Kuren was enough for him, and he wanted no other reward than her gratitude.

"And now, Bruce," said Mr. Van Kuren, "there is a matter of some importance which I wish to discuss with you. Will you please tell me what you know about your father's family, and what sort of a looking man your father was."

Bruce replied as best he could, and then Mr. Van Kuren went on: "Do you remember if your father had a little grey patch on the back of his head?"

"Yes, sir, and so have I," replied the boy readily, as he took off his hat and turned partly around.

Mr. Van Kuren then gazed intently not only at the slight patch of grey, but also at the boy's honest, intelligent face, and continued: "If you had a picture of your father—"

"Why, there's one here, sir," exclaimed Bruce, as he led the way to a large photograph of a group of firemen, in which his father was one.

"There is no sort of a doubt about it," said Mr. Van Kuren as his eye fell upon the portrait of Frank Decker, "and I am very glad to congratulate you, my boy, on your good fortune."

"I wish you would tell me what all this means," exclaimed Bruce excitedly, "for tomorrow I'm going to start for England, and if I have any good fortune I would like to enjoy it at once."

"I can tell you in a very few words my boy" replied Mr. Van Kuren. "Your father's name was Dexter, not Decker. And he was the son of an old gentleman who lives not far from me in the upper part of, the city and whom you have met I believe. Through the cunning and deceit of one of the most treacherous scoundrels whom I have ever known your father became estranged from your grandfather, and I suppose took the name of Decker because he did not wish to have his old friends know what he was doing. He and I were boys together aud although it is more than twenty years since I last saw him, I can readily recognize him in that picture. It was through the merest accident that your grandfather came to suspect your identity and the fact that you can dimly remember the house and grounds uptown, convinces me that you must have been taken there in your early childhood. Very likely your father went up there from time to time in order to re-visit unobserved the scenes of his boyhood. Well, you must come at once for your grandfather is waiting to see you."

To say that Bruce was surprised at what he heard is but a mild way of expressing the sensations that filled his breast as he listened to the words of his father's old friend. It would be nearer the truth to say that he was stunned by the recital. He said nothing however, but put on his coat in a dazed manner and was about to accompany Mr. Van Kuren uptown without even stopping to obtain permission of his superior, when he stopped suddenly and said, "But I am going away to-morrow to England to get a fortune that was left to my father and which through his death has come to me. Perhaps you can tell me what relatives I have over there."

"Relatives in England!" cried Mr. Van Kuren, "I know your family, root and branch, my boy, and you have absolutely no connections in England, that is to say not on your father's side. Who told you about this fortune and advised you to go and get it?"

"I was told about it by a man whose real name I think is Dexter, and who keeps a sort of a loan office in Eldridge Street."

"I think I understand it all now," said Mr. Van Kuren significantly, "that man was the same one who made the trouble between your father and all his friends, and I have no doubt he will be very glad to get you out of the way in order that he may inherit all of your grandfather's property. Did he kindly offer to pay your fare to England?"

"Yes, sir," replied the boy, "and he told me it might be necessary for me to stay there a month or two, during which time he would pay all my expenses."

"Yes, it would serve his purpose very well to get you out of the way for two or three months and then levy blackmail on your grandfather. But thank Heaven there is time to put a stop to that."

"Hey, boss," said a piping voice, and Bruce turned round to find Skinny the Swiper standing beside him with his face and clothes as grimy as if he had been working all night at a fire. He was panting with the exertion of a swift run, and as soon as he could regain his breath he said, "I'was up ter dat hotel fire last night, an' dat Scar-faced Charley got burnt up. Dey jest dragged him outer de ashes an' I seen his body."

"What, dead!" exclaimed Bruce, and then turning to Mr. Van Kuren he said, "that man who wanted me to go to England was burnt up in the big fire last night. I never knew that he lived in that hotel."

"He probably went there when his uncle turned him out of doors," explained Mr. Van Kuren, and then added, "Well, he is dead now and it is best to let his faults be buried with him. We will go up now and see your grandfather."

The meeting between the fine old gentleman and his newly found grandson was an affecting one. Mr. Dexter's eyes brightened and his cheeks flushed when he heard of Bruce's bravery at the fire, and it was with no small pride that he introduced the boy to his friends and the members of his household as his grandson, the son of his dearly beloved son, Frank.

"And now, my boy," said the old gentleman, after they had had a long and affectionate talk together, "if you will go into the drawing room you will find someone there, I think, who wishes to see you."

Bruce did as he was desired, and as he entered the room a young girl rose from her seat by the window and came towards him holding out both hands. "Can you ever forgive me, Bruce, for the way I treated you that day?"

Those who have followed the fortunes of the young fire lad as described in this book do not need to be told that there was no room in his magnanimous heart for any feeling of resentment toward the young girl who stood before him now. Nor is it necessary to say that the whole of the Van Kuren family received Bruce with every manifestation of gratitude and with assurances that henceforth he was to consider himself as one of their own flesh and blood.

But in his new sphere, as the grandson and heir of the aristocratic and kindly old gentleman whose name he was now to bear, Bruce did not forget the friends who had been kind to him during his days of service at the Hook and Ladder quarters. And one of the first things that he did after he had been installed in the big house near the Harlem River was to send substantial tokens of his regard to Chief Trask, Charley Weyman, Tom Brophy and Mr. Dewsnap.

Nor was Skinny the Swiper forgotten. And when the little newsboy started for the Walcott homestead dressed in a neat new suit of clothes and wearing, for perhaps the first time in his life, a new and fashionable hat, very few of those who had associated with him in New York would have recognized him.

"Well," remarked Chief Trask to Tom Brophy as the two sat together at the quarters, "the boy deserves all his good luck, but you mark my words, you'll see him back in the department again before he's a year older. He's just like his father, a fireman born and bred."

THE END.

www.ingramcontent.com/pod-product-compliance
Lightning Source LLC
Chambersburg PA
CBHW051739300426
44115CB00007B/627